The Story of JUDE

The Story of JUDE

❖

A Guide to Rehabilitation Counseling

Sol Mogerman

People with Disabilities Press,
Stanley D. Klein, Ph.D., Series Editor
iUniverse, Inc.
New York Lincoln Shanghai

The Story of JUDE
A Guide to Rehabilitation Counseling

iUniverse, Inc.

For information address:
iUniverse, Inc.
2021 Pine Lake Road, Suite 100
Lincoln, NE 68512
www.iuniverse.com

ISBN: 0-595-31587-9

Printed in the United States of America

For Judy and her Family

Contents

Foreword. xv

Origins xix

Part I   *The Story of JUDE*

Preface 3

Introduction 5

Orientation 8

Session One 11

Session Two 15

Session Three 17

Session Four 18

Session Five. 19

Session Six. 20

Session Seven 22

Session Eight. 23

Session Nine 25

Session Ten. 27

Session Eleven. 29

Session Twelve 31

Session Thirteen 33

Session Fourteen 35

Session Fifteen 37

Session Sixteen 39

Session Seventeen 41

Session Eighteen (Visit with Dr. Keller) 42

Session Nineteen 44

Session Twenty 46

Session Twenty-One 47

Session Twenty-Two 48

Session Twenty-Three 49

Session Twenty-Four 50

Session Twenty-Five 52

Session Twenty-Six 53

Session Twenty-Seven 54

Session Twenty-Eight 55

Session Twenty-Nine 56

Session Thirty 58

Session Thirty-One 60

Session Thirty-Two 61

Session Thirty-Three 63

Session Thirty-Four 66

Session Thirty-Five 68

Session Thirty-Six 70

Session Thirty-Seven 72

Session Thirty-Eight 73

Session Thirty-Nine 75

Session Forty. 77

Session Forty-One. 79

Session Forty-Two 81

Session Forty-Three 83

Session Forty-Four 85

Session Forty-Five. 86

Session Forty-Six. 87

Session Forty-Seven. 89

Session Forty-Eight 91

Session Forty-Nine 92

Session Fifty 94

Session Fifty-One 96

Session Fifty-Two 98

Session Fifty-Three 99

Session Fifty-Four 100

Session Fifty-Five 101

Session Fifty-Six 102

Session Fifty-Seven 103

Session Fifty-Eight 104

Session Fifty-Nine. 106

Probation Meeting 107

Session Sixty 108

Session Sixty-One 110

Session Sixty-Two (Final) 111

Afterword 112

Part II   A Guide to Rehabilitation Counseling

Introduction 117

Chapter 1   The Structure and Nature of Teamwork 118
- *The Formal Structure of Teamwork* *118*
- *The Forgotten Colleagues* *120*

Chapter 2   Colleagues of Physical Relationships 122
- *Doctors* *122*
- *Health Professionals and Technicians* *123*
- *Specialists* *123*
- *Institutional Nurses* *123*
- *Home Care Nurses* *124*
- *Medical Support Workers* *124*
- *Physiotherapists* *125*
- *Alternative Health Practitioners* *125*

Chapter 3   Colleagues of Social Relationships 127
- *Social Workers* *127*
- *Occupational Therapists* *129*
- *Rehabilitation Coordinators* *129*
- *Vocational Counselors/Job Coaches/Specialists* *130*
- *Other Vocational Specialists* *131*
- *Mental Health Professionals and Specialists* *131*
- *Home Care and Support Workers* *132*
- *Lawyers* *133*
- *Law Enforcement Personnel* *133*
- *School Staff and Officials* *134*
- *Non-Profit Societies, Support Groups and Drop-Ins* *135*

Chapter 4   Family 137

- *Parents* *137*
- *Spouses and Partners* *138*
- *Siblings* *139*
- *Children* *140*

Chapter 5   Colleagues of Spiritual Relationships 142

- *Spiritual Leaders/Counselors* *142*
- *Animals, Plants and Nature* *143*
- *Creative Processes* *143*
- *Spiritual Expression* *144*
- *Colleagues of the Past and Other Worlds* *144*

Chapter 6   The Attitudes of a Counselor 145

- *Be Yourself.* *145*
- *Empathy* *145*
- *Unconditional Positive Regard* *146*
- *Undivided Attention* *147*

Chapter 7   Dangers of the Profession 148

- *Competency* *148*
- *Intimacy* *149*
- *Power* *150*

Chapter 8   The Building of Rapport 151

- *Your Input into the Building of Rapport* *151*
- *Your Client's Input to Building and Maintaining Rapport* *152*
- *Rapport in the Chemistry of Relationship* *152*

Chapter 9   Counseling Skills 153

- *Listening* *153*
- *Observing* *155*
- *Reflection.* *157*
- *Role Playing and Immediacy.* *157*
- *Pacing and Matching* *157*
- *Synthesizing.* *159*

Chapter 10   The Counseling Environment. 160
- *Institutional Settings*. *160*
- *Office Environments*. *161*
- *In the Client's Home*. *162*

Chapter 11   Care of the Counselor 163
- *Revisiting the Attitudes of Counseling*. *163*
- *Grieve Your Losses* *164*
- *Do Things That Feel Good* *164*

Chapter 12   Hopes and Dreams 165
- *Stay in Touch*. *165*
- *The Relationship Lives on in Spirit* *165*

REFERENCES 166
- *References for Process Oriented Memory Resolution* *168*
- *References for Response Based Therapy* *168*

About the Author 169
Index 171

Acknowledgements

I would like to acknowledge the following persons for their contributions to this work: Rob (for trusting me to tell his sister's story), Peter and Wendy (for sharing their knowledge and love of Jude), Nancy and Sandy of the Insurance Corporation of British Columbia (for supporting my relationship with Jude), Stan Klein (for publication of this book), Richard Routledge (for copy-editing), Diane Davis (for early editing of story), Karen Graham (for manuscript preparation), Bruce, Laurel, and Leanne (for giving it a read and getting back to me), Dale Dunham (for cover photography), Bryan Wilson (for author photo), Lennon-McCartney (for lyrics to "Hey Jude"), Barry Mogerman (for being my brother and taking more than his share of the load), and most of all my wife, Gundula Mogerman (for her beautiful drawing, astute and inspired editing, and unconditional giving of herself to all phases of creating this book).

Foreword

If you rolled into a strange town late at night with a tired spouse, two grumpy children in the back of your broken down car and no money for a motel or food, Sol Mogerman is the guy you would want to meet. Sol is not a professional mechanic, although he could probably fix your car if it was more than twenty years old. If not, he would find a good mechanic who would work cheap. He might not give you money, but he would help you find a clean, safe place for the night. And he would be sure to round up some snacks for the kids.

Sol would want to know where you came from, how you managed to get as far as you did, and where you wanted to go. While you waited on the repairs, he would ensure that the town became a place to you, with friendly locals and funky side streets. You would learn a bit about Sol as well; not anything you did not want to know, but enough to realize that he was a fellow traveler who at times had also relied on the good will of strangers. Once you hit the road again you would probably find yourself feeling a bit more hopeful about people. And when you got home you would have a great story to tell, about a breakdown that turned into something else altogether.

Rehabilitation counseling is a specialized field of work. The client is often highly vulnerable. She may be suffering the loss of herself, in the sense that she cannot participate in the world as she used to, and the loss of her most important relationships—in Jude's case, her children. Disabling physical or cognitive injuries may expose her to social judgments and exclusion. Unable to command the simple respect she once routinely expected and received, she may be objectified by medical, mental health, and social service practitioners. She may be unable to keep up with the rapid micro-level exchanges that comprise every day conversation and consequently feel alone even in the company of good friends.

She may find herself living in relative poverty at the whim of an insurance company whose primary concern is limiting its exposure. Her physical safety may also be compromised. For instance, I recently worked for a woman who suffered a brain injury and could not at first recall that her husband was physically and verbally abusive and that, just prior to the accident, she had been planning to leave him. The unique long-term challenges facing such individuals require equally unique responses from their counselors.

The Story of Jude is the book on rehabilitation counseling Carl Rogers would have written had he gained the depth of understanding Sol has acquired from the experience of his own head injury. It contains an unusually detailed account of a complex and ultimately successful counselor-client relationship, and a set of principles for the practice of rehabilitation counseling. In keeping with the spirit of rehabilitation counseling, the book is highly accessible and practical. The writing is clear, direct, and virtually jargon-free—no mean feat for a book on counseling. As a result, Jude's circumstances and the key events in the counseling practice strike the reader directly, with an immediacy that is at times arresting.

The book conveys in simple, poignant terms the profound psychological distress and social problems Jude suffered in the aftermath of her accident and at the whim of Huntington's disease. But we immediately see and never lose sight of Jude's courage. Sol shows us that Jude possesses her own history and dreams for the future, her own ideas and techniques for getting through the day, and her own creative and sometimes strident ways of asserting her basic human dignity. As in all good counseling, it is the client who emerges as the primary force in her own recovery.

Sol deliberately downplays the technical aspects of his approach, not out of false modesty, but because he wants to maintain a focus on the client's resourcefulness and does not want the counselor-client relationship reduced to a set of techniques. Nevertheless, the book contains many clear illustrations of basic and advanced counseling skills. It gives fresh meaning to fuzzy concepts like "authenticity", "congruency," and "unconditional positive regard" that are too often tossed about as clichés. One particularly important contribution of the book, in my view, is Sol's illustration of creative reminiscence, the collaborative process through which the client experiences and integrates aspects of her pre-injury self as a foundation for the development of a new, post-injury self.

For Sol, the technical aspects of rehabilitation counseling are superseded by a set of ethically and spiritually informed attitudes: a willingness to immerse himself in the client's world; a desire to learn from the client, and be changed; a keen eye for the myriad small ways in which the client exerts her basic dignity; an alertness to the most subtle forms of self expression; an ever present sense of humour; a playful irreverence for orthodoxies of virtually any kind; a readiness to persist through difficult times; a delight in having his own preconceptions exposed as false; a focus on what works; a respectful curiosity; an appreciation for the client's quirks and eccentricities, and his own; an inclusive approach to other helpers; and a deep sense of trust in the client.

Allan Wade Ph.D.
Duncan, British Columbia
Canada

Origins

Many of the theories, practices, and teachings that influenced me in the counseling of Jude have come through my education, readings, and contact with friends and colleagues. My education exposed me to the works of Richard Bandler and John Grinder, Albert Ellis, Eric H. Erikson, Milton H. Erikson, Sigmund Freud, C.G. Jung, Rollo May, Jean Piaget, Carl Rogers, Elizabeth Kubler-Ross, Virginia Satir, Irwin Yalom, and other contributors to the field of counseling and psychology. Much of this exposure was through texts and instructors who managed to make the theories and ideas alive for me.

Some of my teachers have been those who have shared with me important influences in their careers at precisely the most opportune moment for my best understanding. These individuals include Bob Corley, Joan Costello, Kirk Hewitt, Terry Higgins, Tim Mack, Ralph Maddess, Rod Punnett, Richard Routledge, and Jeff Smith.

I would also like to express gratitude to Dr. Mariko Tanaka and Dr. Allan Wade for their theories of "Process Oriented Memory Resolution" and "Response Based Therapy" respectively. These theories helped to make me aware that trauma is imprinted in the very core of our experience and is accessible for healing through a therapeutic drawing out of the fundamentally healthy response in our pre-traumatic moment. Dr. Tanaka uses varying techniques to recreate traumatic memory and reframe it, along with the faulty belief systems surrounding it, using the wisdom of the pre-damaged psyche to inform healing. Dr. Wade informs healing through employing a carefully chosen use of language and detailed exploration of a person's *responses* to uncover innate resistance to the oppression of traumatic experience. These two originators and their ideas have enhanced my awareness of human nature and changed my understanding and practice of counseling for the better.

Then there are my mentors who have infused me with their greatness and encouraged me to create and produce from the depths of my own true origin. They include Sveva Caetani, Raymond Miller, Henry Schaefer-Simmern, and Dr. Reidar Wennesland.

In this work the astute student of counseling may see correlation to many of the theoretical originators mentioned above, and elsewhere, and wonder why they are not cited at the precise moment of recognition. This is because their work has influenced me in such a manner that I have incorporated it into the very fabric of my being. Consequently it feels unnatural to cite references during the flow of my narrative. I have included references in this book to provide you with links to specific readings of some of those who have most influenced my work. These include writers, thinkers, and artists within and without the field of counseling and can be found on page 166.

I would be remiss not to mention the spiritual teachings that have shaped my essential relationship with the world and my self. These teachings include legacies of Jewish, Christian, Native American, Hindu, and Buddhist influence and have quickened my openness to their edification through contact with sacred texts and true followers. I am fortunate to have encountered both on my path.

PART I
The Story of JUDE

"But we—you and I and those of our kin, we penitents, seekers after truth and fugitives from the world—are not innocent, and cannot be brought to order by thundering sermons."

—**Hermann Hesse,** *Magister Ludi 1949*

Preface

The exchange of energy between Jude Banks and myself over a year and a half of counseling therapy, where she was the client and I the counselor, produced results that noticeably changed the quality of her life for the better. Jude overcame seemingly insurmountable loss and bitterness to triumph in the end as a clear and emotionally healthy person.

Colleagues and people who knew Jude before and after her therapy asked me *how* I did it. This was an inquiry that I dared not directly answer, as the question of *how* I or the tools of my profession actually *do* anything that produces observable results is extremely complicated and obscured by the chemistry of human relationship. I believe one answer to the above question might be found on the interpretive side of the border between observable fact and creative inference. Therefore I have chosen to respond by writing my answer in the form of a story of our time together. I do, however, feel a further responsibility to highlight my thoughts, as a counselor, during its telling. The attitudes, skills and philosophies behind my work treating survivors of brain injury and trauma are discussed in Part II of this book.

It is my finding that the most devastating result of trauma and disability is its negative effect on self-image. Self-image, or how we see ourselves, is reliant upon the seemingly indisputable knowledge that our innate talents and abilities define us and are essential to the status of our relationship with others. When this knowledge is compromised, we lose the ability to see our place in the world and are vulnerable to a profound and devastating loss of self.

Consequently it is imperative that any meaningful therapy of rehabilitation consciously addresses the loss and restoration of self-image as a most essential component of psychological health. I believe that this can be achieved through the combination of *creative reminiscence* and *the grieving process*.

Using *creative reminiscence* the counselor guides a client to re-experience intact parts of the old self-image in order to provide a foundation for the integration of a new one. This is accomplished by drawing out these parts through the re-creation, in therapy, of pre-trauma exploits and experiences using any number of therapeutic devices including story-telling, role-play, art, music, writing, and body work. It is vital, in the employment of the latter therapies, to carefully balance the craft of counseling with the art of friendship, for a positive self-image can only be nourished when abilities are validated and reflected *in* a congenial *relationship* with another.

Inevitably, survivors of trauma and disability will experience grief over the loss of their abilities and it is the counselor's task to help them acknowledge and process this grief through the *grieving process*. The *grieving process* draws out emotions that provide an opportunity to re-live and relieve loss through the random expression of anger, sadness, fear, shock, guilt, denial and hope.

When coupled with *the grieving process*, *creative reminiscence* helps to create the memory (story) for a loss, and provides someone (the counselor) to share the grief with. I have found that the serendipitous nature of spontaneous and unrehearsed communication creates an ideal environment for the use of *creative reminiscence* and *the grieving process*. This is because both aspects of therapy are most effective if the right component of a client's story is made accessible when he or she is most receptive to its therapeutic influence. Therefore it is important that the relationship between client and counselor remain as flexible and spontaneous as possible within the boundaries of the profession.

The following story is based on my session notes and told with the client's permission. Names and places have been changed to protect confidentiality.

Introduction

A good year after our final session, Jude's Huntington's disease had progressed to the degree that she was losing her balance, falling down, and injuring herself at home often enough to consider leaving her sweet little house for safer and more physically supportive surroundings. She voluntarily applied for and received residence at the same extended care hospital facility that her brother Wade lived in. I visited her there a couple of times after her move from her old home. These hospital visits found her cheerful, responsive, smoke free, and well kept, however her ability to communicate verbally appeared to be rapidly degenerating until, at our most recent meeting, it was so eroded that I was barely able to understand her. This may have been due to the fact that her disease was jarring her so violently that she didn't have time to form words without unmerciful interruption, or simply because I was out of practice with her mode of speech.

She nevertheless did manage to put across her most important message to me through dogged repetition of the words "HEALTHY," "YOU MADE HEART," "HEALTHY,"—along with hugging me and making gestures of holding her heart. I was at first compelled to practice the modesty of my profession and replied that we had "done it together", but she would not accept this premise and kept urgently repeating "HEALTHY," "YOU MADE HEART," "HEALTHY." In spite of my professional inclination, I eventually gratefully acknowledged her hard won communication as the unquestionable expression of her deepest truth.

After all, isn't that what counseling is all about—*witnessing the sanctity of each other's reality?* I personally believe that my clients are gazing into my soul with the same intensity and curiosity that I gaze into theirs. If this were not allowed, I would be the first to do away with being called a "counselor" altogether. Consequently I count my clients among my best friends and love them as fully as I am able. This does not necessarily mean that I bring them home for dinner (my family won't let me), but it does demand my full attention and focus in the reciprocal dance of our being together.

In my understanding, counseling is not running clients through a predetermined course of therapy designed to solve their problems, but about the *living relationship* between the counselor and client in an environment where each is fundamentally equal with the other. In this environment it is the *responsibility* of the counselor to create an atmosphere that encourages a reflection of the client's sacred knowledge of his or her self in order to better utilize energy found in the natural healing process. The creation of such an ambiance was at the heart of the relationship between Jude Banks and myself that began in July of 1998.

Jude came to me with a dual diagnosis of Huntington's disease and acquired brain injury. The Huntington's came from her genes and the brain injury from being struck down by a car. The attendant losses resulting from both of these sources created a third and profoundly influential psychological condition of overwhelming grief.

Huntington's is a hereditary disease that has a 50/50 chance of being passed from parent to child. It is at present an incurable, though medically manageable, progressive condition resulting from cumulative damage to the nervous system. It often shows up in a person's thirties or forties and can last from ten to thirty years. The disease is usually characterized by difficulties in three areas: a movement disorder, dementia, and psychiatric disturbances.

The "movement disorder" is called "Chorea" from the Greek word for "dance." It takes the form of involuntary movements and produces jerky gyrations that flow randomly from one part of the body to another. This creates clumsiness and problems with speech and walking. At 40, Jude was manifesting these disabling physical symptoms and needed assistance with some of her activities of daily living. The movement disorder also causes excessive weight loss from calories burnt in constant movement and problems with swallowing.

In the context of Huntington's disease, "dementia" is referred to as a loss in intellectual abilities, such as memory, concentration, problem solving, and judgment. A loss in these abilities is also associated with acquired brain injury and at the beginning it was difficult, if not impossible, to distinguish which of Jude's "intellectual losses," if any, were attributable to brain injury and which to Huntington's disease. During my time with her I found Jude to be an innately bright and intelligent woman, with a reasonably good memory, who sometimes manifested eccentric modes of problem solving and childlike judgment. These eccentricities simply proved to be part of her personality and did not preclude her ability to create and maintain meaningful relationships with the world—so I never really questioned her ability to do so. Therefore I had no interest in curing Jude of what might be diagnosed as "dementia."

"Psychiatric disturbances" from Huntington's disease usually, but not always, take the form of depression, paranoia, hostility, mania, and obsessive-compulsive symptoms. These conditions, often associated with brain injury, *are also found in those who have suffered great losses.* Combined with the physical losses associated with Huntington's disease and psychological disorientation generated by brain injury, Jude had lost a beloved partner, the care of her children, her autonomy, and her sense of safety. These staggering losses, especially the loss of caring for her children, united to create an overpowering state of grief. As a counselor I chose to concentrate my therapeutic efforts on helping Jude grieve her multiple losses and reestablish what proved to be her pre-injury self-image as a functional mother and gracious friend.

It turned out that this remarkable woman equated the image of her completed healing with that of a spiritually healthy heart. She endowed me with magical powers, called me "Santa", and saw me with childlike eyes. She challenged me by literally asking me to "heal her heart." She had faith that I could. I knew better than to believe myself capable of doing this exclusively through a textbook employment of the tools of my profession, so *I infused the image of healing her heart into my every purposeful action with her.*

The following is not a thesis on the relationship between emotional expression and the manifestations of Huntington's disease and brain injury. It is not about Jude or myself, but about *our relationship* during the one-and-a-half years of our journey together through the dark, disturbing, sometimes hopeless, and ulti-mately forgiving path of her restoration.

I hope that sharing my thoughts as a counselor during our time together will help demystify the therapeutic process, and give you a ringside seat in a world of healing so subtle and intimate that it cannot be adequately expressed in a simple case history. Jude is a real person. I am a real person. Her family, friends, and helpers are real people. Together we were magic.

Orientation

What did I know about Huntington's disease? Not much, except the memory of a photograph of Bob Dylan sitting by Woody Gutherie's bedside in a hospital back East. In that photograph Guthrie, who had Huntington's, looked wan and hollow. I had no idea what he looked like at any other time during the course of his illness, nor would have been able to recognize his symptoms if I had seen them displayed on the street.

What did I know about brain injury? Plenty. I am a survivor of a brain injury, and make my living, counseling brain injured clients for the rehabilitation department of an insurance company in British Columbia, Canada. This work makes great demands on my powers of empathy and technical skills as a counselor. I was definitely interested when I received the call from a coordinator to begin work with Jude Banks, a reputedly difficult and challenging client who had recently burned out and fired a number of the people hired to help her.

The coordinator told me that Jude had Huntington's disease in addition to a brain injury, and sent me post-accident medical and professional reports to bring me up to speed on her condition. These reports presented a diagnosis of injury that was greatly complicated by the virtually unanswerable question of how to distinguish the influence of Huntington's disease upon brain injury—and *vice versa*. A question that not only intrigued me but made me want to meet Jude and experience this enigmatic combination of symptoms for myself.

I knew that my almost non-existent knowledge of Huntington's disease was not a very promising beginning for a scientific investigation. Fortunately my job was not solely to distinguish the symptoms in question but to help Jude recover from her accident inflicted brain injury and interact more harmoniously with her world. It was also suggested that I meet with two members of the present and recently fired team to familiarize myself with her case.

A conference was set up at a restaurant, and as I drove to my meeting I mused about what I could really learn about someone through the perceptions of others. The team members I was to confer with were officially designated as "support workers."

I was met at a homey restaurant by Sandy, the recently fired, and Paul, the inheritor of her position. They chose a table that put us a bit too close together. Sandy thrust her face, lined with anguish, at me and began by offering a detailed handwritten diary of her every hour with my new client. I flipped through the pages wondering about the difficulty of trying to decipher her loopy blue script, gratefully accepted the book, and gave it back after it sat unread on my desk for a number of months. Curiosity, mixed with impatience, increased my desire to meet Jude in person so that I could form my own opinions about her.

All I knew, so far, were inconclusive conjectures of puzzling reports, and the fact that Jude had fired Sandy for throwing away precious keepsakes during a recent move to a new apartment. Apparently Jude had discovered Sandy's culls next to a dumpster and had to be talked out of posting a 24 hour guard over them by Paul who feared for her health if she spent the night sitting with no blanket on frozen ground. He convinced her to stand guard in the house, where she could protect the rest of her belongings before they were spirited away outside. Sandy, deeply hurt and apologetic, denied any wrongdoing in the dumpster affair. Jude's rage at her was so stunning and complete that there seemed little hope for reconciliation.

During lunch I learned that Sandy was only one on a hit list of people Jude hated with relentless energy and passion. This list included her doctor, lawyer, the judge who had signed the order to take her children away, her ex-husband and his partner, the man who ran her down with his car, the welfare department, and her younger brother who was also her legal guardian. Jude had elaborate schemes for punishing each person she perceived to have hurt her. The judge was scheduled to have a bag of dog excrement dumped on his desk and her ex-husband and most of the others could expect not so cordial visits from the Hells Angels, whom she claimed were at her beck and call. No one took these threats too literally, but some eyebrows, or nostrils, were starting to be raised as a paper bag of dog droppings grew fuller on her front door stoop.

The people on Jude's list were bitterly hated for specific reasons—each bearing, in her mind, some responsibility for the loss of her status as an independent homemaker and caretaker of her own children. Even Sandy's alleged mistreatment of her personal objects was translated into contributing to that all-consuming loss. Jude was so distraught over her losses that she had been recently discovered night walking down the middle of a rainy highway, against traffic, in a bid to regain control over her destiny through ending her miserable life.

Paul informed me of the delicate balance of Jude's emotional stability, and warned that it was relatively easy to slip and commit unintentional insult to her tenuous sense of autonomy. He also mentioned that she was very well known and loved in the community for her out-going personality coupled with a good and generous nature. Both Paul and Sandy described Jude as an exceptionally sweet and loving person. They also apprised me of her tendency to be very physically demonstrative with hugs and kisses.

Sandy left after lunch and I had coffee with Paul, and waited until it was time for me to follow him to Jude's and be introduced as her new counselor. He filled me in with stories and anecdotes that led me to believe that I was about to meet someone who was larger than life.

Session One

Paul pulled up in front of a run down housing block, got out, and walked me to the door of a ground floor unit carelessly obstructed by random junk, cardboard boxes, and stacks of empty beer and pop cans. A grimy white vinyl curtain sagged across smeared glass patio doors that served as a front entrance to the living room and kitchen of Jude's apartment. The yard was a narrow strip of clumpy grass strewn with cigarette butts and a couple of scraggly trees. The stuff piled in front of her door competed for green space and created a barrier to easy ingress.

Paul climbed over the barricade and pounded on the glass door with his fist trying to be heard over the roar of a turned up television. In response to his efforts, the vinyl curtain eventually twitched, folded, and parted to reveal a weathered arm that jerked the sliding door open enough to allow the emergence of a cloud of stale blue tobacco smoke. She emerged from within. Beautiful, slender dancing pixie in a grubby gray sweat suit, flailing her bangled arms and swaying like a loose-jointed rag doll. I was astonished, and stepped back a bit. Paul introduced me, rather formally, as "Sol" her "new counselor."

Jude took one look at me through winky eyes, gave an open stump-toothed smile, and proclaimed "Angel Santa Claus!" Then she threw her arms around my neck, pulled me closer, tried to kiss me on the mouth, and playfully tugged at my beard with tobacco stained fingers. I felt like a lifesaver in her storm. It took some doing to unwind her arms and reclaim my personal space. After she settled down, Paul drove off and left us alone for our first session, which lasted for an hour and a half.

We squeezed around the junk into the living room of her apartment, which allowed for little furniture due to the piles of meaningful objects that took up three-quarters of the space and spilled out onto every available surface. It looked impossible to cook on the range, because the burners were covered with keepsakes including photographs, cards, trinkets, and crumbling art projects.

Each and every object seemed to provide a vital link to Jude's loved ones and had its inviolable place in her shrine. It was obvious to me how anyone who threatened to disturb these links was violating her sacred objects and would certainly become a target of her rage. Gingerly sliding around the edges of the shrine, we slipped onto a sagging couch and wonky chair that threatened to dump me on the floor if I leaned back at all.

Jude smoked incessantly during our interview, dropping ashes and live coals onto the couch and rug in spite of her attempts to use a heaping ashtray. She had strict rituals around her smoking that included saying "light my fire" whenever she lit up, which was literally one after the other. Because of the Huntington's disease, Jude's arms were always in motion and I developed the technique of bracing my hand against hers to ensure a proper light. After I lit her cigarette, she would say "Thank you Babe" and wait for me to deliberately hand back her plastic *Bic* lighter.

Lighting Jude's cigarettes in this manner promoted familiarity and seemed to make her feel like a respectable lady who was being tended by a gentleman. It also gave me the opportunity to measure the shaking of her hand against mine and the lability, if any, of her disease over time. Return of the lighter was also essential to building and maintaining trust and became an important ritual that I performed exactly the same way, carefully putting it back in her hand, hundreds of times over the course of our many sessions.

The apartment rug bore countless black-fringed holes and I often wondered how she hadn't burnt the place down yet. Jude seemed to make no effort to protect the furniture and rug from burning ashes, other than providing the occasional overflowing ashtray, which she flicked at with little control and a distracted sense of duty.

I reasoned that the flailing motions of her disease were responsible for many of the burn holes in the rug. I also came to understand that she must have truly hated and disrespected her apartment. This may have been because she was moved there against her will after the break up of the cherished home she used to share with her children and Huntington's afflicted older brother Wade. I was curious to see how she would care for a place that she liked, because she was referred to, in some of the pre-injury reports I had read, as "not the best housekeeper."

After we settled on the scary furniture, Jude wanted to get to work right away and laid out the main points of her problem.

First she acknowledged how hard it was to have Huntington's disease by telling me that it literally wore her out to be involuntarily moving around all the time. She called it "dancing" and referred to herself as a "happy dancer." Then she told me, not so happily, how sad and painful her life was without her children and that she would very much like *me* to cure her of her problems.

It occurred to me that having a client associate me with Santa Claus might create a situation that put me dangerously close to being seen as an "omnipotent healer." This situation was well warned against in my professional training, as a potentially unhealthy imbalance of power. As a result I realized that I had better set up some boundaries with my new client and limit my status to that of a mortal friend and helper.

I carefully told her that I was her counselor and my name was "Sol." She repeated my name, "Soller." As it turned out, Jude continued to call me "Santa," but did remember, with some prompting, that my real name was "Sol." When I later spoke of my wife she dubbed her "Mrs. Santa" and developed a burning curiosity about meeting my family. I told her that my kids were grown and that my wife and I lived together with a big black dog.

I figured that it was helpful in the recovery of her self-image, as a functional mother and housekeeper, to relate to me as a family oriented friend who had experienced similar concerns and responsibilities. From that point on the first thing Jude would often say to me when I showed up for her counseling sessions was "Hi Hon, how's your Angel family?" I always took a couple of minutes to answer her questions and tell her what was new with my family. She would answer appropriately with news about her own that usually consisted of supervised visits with Paul and her youngest son. Sometimes she would have new additions to the shrine to show me when she was given cards or artwork.

Jude told me over and over that she had a "broken heart," a theme that was to stay at the forefront of our work together for the next year and a half. She deeply grieved having her children removed from her care, and may have related to it as a painful repetition of the childhood break-up of her own family when she was a child. Besides the loss of her family, she expressed distress over being sexually abused as a little girl. The theme of her abuse was brought up again as she grappled with her responses to being sexually harassed by strangers she met on the street.

Jude preferred to deal with this harassment in a situation specific vigilante manner by carrying a large carpenter's hammer, to ward off attackers, concealed in a rubber boot on her walker. I never heard of her having to use this weapon on anyone and she preferred not to delve into the darkness of her childhood abuse when I asked her to elaborate.

The main expression of her grief was rage at those who had anything to do with the removal of her children from her care. She was to repeat the lament "I sure miss my Angel kids" many, many times over the course of our sessions. She also often mourned the loss of her partner, "Crazy Bill," who was killed in a motorcycle accident. She remembered Bill to me as a loving and supportive man with whom she shared a rich and full life. He died when she was pregnant with her youngest son, Jamie. Bill's untimely death put an abrupt end to a long chapter of happiness in her life. In fact, it was some years later, while she was mourning this loss, at the very intersection where Crazy Bill was killed, that she was struck down by a car and sustained her brain injury.

Jude readily acknowledged that she had lost herself "somewhere in the brain injury." She blamed this event for losing control of her life and having her beloved children taken away.

Jude's feeling of loss of control was augmented by the degenerative nature of her Huntington's disease and the court's opinion that she was no longer capable of caring for herself or others. As a result of this judgment her younger brother, John, became her legal guardian. Jude resented John's control over her life and put him on her list of enemies claiming that all he wanted was to "rip off" the money she would receive in her pending lawsuit with the insurance company against the man who ran her over.

In our first meeting, Jude presented me with a comprehensive outline of her enemies and losses, and gave herself to me to help her find her way to health. The communication between us was so intense that I wrote in my session notes:

> "Each time I make a connection with her there is a light between us and she grounds her spirit with mine. It is my job to do this over and over until that light becomes a reality for her. It takes a tremendous amount of energy to work with Jude for she feels a spiritual grounding more profoundly through people than things and all the people she loves have been removed from her life. In the midst of her wide dance is a center of incredible sweetness. Her energy is not broad, but clear and precise. She knows exactly what she wants and is desperately trying to take back control of her world. Her paranoia and delusions of just retribution against those she perceives responsible for ruining her life seem, to me, to be nothing more than natural manifestations of her grief."

Session Two

Jude reminisced about life before her accident, when she rented a 2,000 square foot home in the country with Bill, the children, and lots of family pets. She described a happy, easygoing lifestyle that centered on her ability to be a good wife, loving mother, caretaker, and gracious friend. Again Jude was very adamant that her accident related brain injury created a distinct line for the before and after of her happiness. "Before my brain injury things were great! Now, my heart is broken."

After she acknowledged her pain, Jude went on to rant about how angry she felt when home care workers mistreated her things; especially gifts from her children. It was as if the workers had actually touched an exposed nerve whenever they disturbed the sanctity of her shrine.

People she liked, she called "Angel," but those she felt hurt by she called "Asshole." This appellation would readily enter her language and she would refer to people she was furious with by attaching that derogatory term to their names in my conversations with her. I came to know these people as "Asshole Brent" (ex-husband), "Asshole Mara" (Brent's wife), "Asshole Sandy"(ex-home support worker), "Asshole John"(younger brother and conservator), "Asshole Lawyer," "Asshole Judge," "Asshole Doctor," "Asshole Social Worker,"…etc.

Jude was sad and angry about her losses and I encouraged her to express these feelings as much as possible. Once I started clucking the word "fuck" "fuck fuck fuck fuck fuck fuck fuck.!," hoping she would follow and express her frustration without specifically directing it at another person. She was eager to join me and took off squawking "fuck!" for several minutes. It was like bleeding off a volcano. I actually had a bit of a time trying to quiet her down.

After this release she had no trouble telling me, in a relatively calm manner, how sad she was about losing her children and how angry she felt at those she perceived to be responsible for taking them away from her.

I always made it my business to get Jude's full attention and permission whenever I removed an object from the shrine. I meticulously replaced every stuffed toy, trinket, doll, photo, plastic flower, or card exactly as I found it. My exploration of her sacred objects was often done at her bidding when she wanted to share something that one of her kids had given to her, or for therapeutic reasons when I thought they might evoke important stories of her past/pre-injury identity.

As we became more comfortable with each other, I allowed some disclosure, on my part, of how sad and angry I felt about the life I lost as a result of my own catastrophic accident and brain injury of 13 years earlier. Jude empathized immediately and, after briefly hearing my story, pegged the greatest aspect of my loss as that of my ability to play music—which was very true.

She also acknowledged and empathized with my hatred towards the town in which I was injured because, she confided, she felt the same way about the town in which she was injured. Jude's sympathetic camaraderie showed me that, no matter how often she mentioned them, she was not completely consumed by her own troubles.

Often clients like to get involved in their therapists' lives as a ploy to avoid working on their own. Jude's ability to express her own woes and sympathize with mine revealed that she was able to both work on her own problems and relate to me as a comforting friend—something that was integral to the person she identified as herself before her injury. It was becoming clear to me that *a great part of my work with Jude was the reestablishment of her experiencing herself as a compassionate and gracious friend.*

Throughout our sessions, Jude was constantly touching and caressing my arm, tugging at my beard and rubbing my belly, which made me distinctly uneasy in terms of the maintenance of my professional boundaries with her. I felt the need to establish the fact that I was a married man and not available to her as anything other than a friend and counselor. It also occurred to me that her demonstrativeness might be a by-product of her peculiar mix of Huntington's disease and brain injury. Maybe she was hanging on to me to ground herself through contact with my body? If this were so, I was gratified at the level of trust and rapport that allowed her to use me for grounding.

Session Three

When I came to see Jude at 1 o'clock, as arranged, she was not home and I feared she might be developing the pattern of missing appointments that she had shown with a previous psychologist. I hung out in town and doubled back past her place later to see if she was in. She was, and seemed relieved to see me.

Jude was full of news that the landlord had "evicted" her from her apartment because she had been playing her radio too loudly at night. She was also in trouble for swearing at him when he came over to inform her that he had turned off her power for the rest of the night. The altercation must have triggered her grief over having lost her previously secure and happy home, and unleashed the emotion (rage) that she most readily used to express her feelings of vulnerability and loss.

Jude did not perceive her "eviction" in itself as an immediate threat and was probably secretly pleased that she might be forced to move from her hated apartment to a better place. In light of this possibility, she was not terribly distressed about an impending move. She was however much more upset over the loss of her children and expressed that she wanted to move to the country where she could have her family back again. Her hopes to rent or buy a country home were somewhat unrealistic and evidence of her great desire and need to reclaim her old status and identification as a parent and homemaker.

Once Jude got going on the loss of her children more anger and sadness came into play. She was very clear about what she had lost and was able to articulate it as "The ability to mother my children—*probably the only real job I ever had!*"

Over and over, for a year and a half she acknowledged and expressed her great loss. She never seemed to tire of it and I thought the more she was able to express it, the better. During this session Jude pushed my boundaries, repeatedly calling me "Santa" and literally trying to sit in my lap. I told her that only my pets and grandchildren were allowed to sit in my lap and encouraged her to be intimate by sharing with me how she felt. She seemed to get the idea without being hurt and we continued to examine how she experienced herself before and after her brain injury. I asked her to think about Crazy Bill and remember some stories about him to tell me for next time.

Session Four

I was gratified to see that Jude had done her homework from our previous session, and that she was bursting with stories about her life with Crazy Bill. She told me that Bill took care of her and how their life was full and exciting. They had a rambling place near the ocean with an overgrown yard and lots of room for the kids to play. She described the thrill of riding behind Bill on his big blue and gold Harley. The Harley was also fondly remembered as a family vehicle when it was attached to a homemade sidecar.

To make Bill more real, Jude brought my attention to the tattered photograph of a shirtless, tattooed, longhaired, bearded man with sunglasses sitting on a couch in cut-off jeans. It was difficult to see his features because the photograph was so crumpled and stained—with tears?

As we talked and Jude grieved, she seemed to become more and more solid. Her language grew increasingly descriptive and she savored the details of her story-telling. She had gone from only being able to call herself the "lonely boss" to feeling more connected with her past as she allowed herself to explore her memories.

Grieving Bill also brought out her acute longing for companionship and she started to physically harass me and tried to climb in my lap as we sat on the couch. When I stood up to evade her, she withdrew to the chair and her Huntington's movements virtually ceased, leaving her in quiet to mourn.

When she recovered, Jude remembered Crazy Bill "coming home on his Harley" from his work as a tow truck operator, with a big bag of groceries between his legs. This memory evoked the experience of perfect marital bliss and had at its core the expressed sentiment that "Bill took care of everything!" She even postulated that, though he was dead, Bill was going to "take care of the guy who ran me down."

Session Five

Jude started off by only telling me that she was "lonely." This singular lament was a change from her usual litany of how she missed her children. She also expressed that she missed living with other people. When I asked "What people?" she responded by saying "Jesus people."

She didn't elaborate on what she meant by "Jesus people" and immediately changed the subject to tell me about the night she was hit by the car that caused her brain injury. There seemed to be an urgency in her need to talk about the particulars of her accident, yet she was short of details and could only repeat over and over, "it really happened…it really happened…it really happened."…like she was trying to convince herself of its reality. If Jude could not remember the accident itself, I thought she might remember the incidents that led up to it.

When I asked, all she remembered was being in a coffee shop with some friends and, not feeling like company, excusing herself early to spend time outside on the very corner where Bill had been killed on his motorcycle. Next, she struggled to recount how she thought she saw or heard the car approach her, but had to concede that she had no real memory of being hit. Like many of my trauma-induced brain-injured clients, she only remembered waking up in the hospital.

The effort of trying to remember her accident curiously seemed to calm her down, and by the time she had exhausted her resources for verbal recall, her Huntington's movements had noticeably slowed down. Then she told me she could never really be at peace until her "heart was fixed." Each time she brought this up I rededicated myself to realizing the core mission of our work together: the healing of her heart.

Session Six

A meeting with Jude's lawyer last week brought me face to face with the problem he was having assessing her losses in quantifiable terms. Though it was not one of my concerns as a therapist, the lawyer's need to define Jude's capacity to earn money before her injuries seemed somehow linked to my post-injury quest to help her regain her self-image as a functional person. With this in mind I chose to question Jude about her employment history.

She was very forthcoming and quickly warmed to the subject. It gave her the opportunity to give me some details of life with her first husband, Rick Banks, whom she left because he didn't want to have children with her. I asked if this was because he was aware of the risk of their children inheriting her Huntington's disease, and she answered, a bit evasively, that Rick "just didn't want to have kids."

Jude's relationship with Rick contradicted her belief at 18, that "you got married and had kids." Memories of her employment included Rick picking her up for lunch from her job as a clerk at a building supply center. He would drive by, when she was outside, yell "Hey You!" and then take her home for a "nooner." At that time, home was at Rick's parents, "Ma and Pa" Banks who took Rick and Jude in when they needed a place to live.

Jude fondly remembered Rick and seemed to have no rancor at him or qualms at having left him to find another man to father her children. Evidence of her attachment to her first marriage was her retention of the name "Banks," in spite of her subsequent marriage and the opportunity to reclaim her maiden name. She informed me that she had a "big hippy wedding" with Rick and asked if I wanted to see the blue wedding dress that she said she still had, but didn't produce when I showed interest. I assumed it must have been buried under too much memorabilia to be easily accessible and didn't pursue a showing.

Talking about this happy time in her life made Jude less flighty and more solid. Her mind and speech seemed to flow easier as she recounted her life with Rick.

Experiencing the movements of Jude's Huntington's disease on a weekly basis over time gave me the opportunity to observe how differences in her emotional state corresponded to the frequency and intensity of specific body movements. Having said this one could infer, at this stage of her disease, that the involuntary movements of Jude's body might also have changed in some appreciable manner during the ebb and flow of everyday emotional lability. In my experience this was not evident and the only observable variations in her movements, other than those linked to changes in medication, seemed connected with reminiscence, and especially, the specific emotional output of directly grieving her losses.

During our time spent mourning a particular loss or set of losses, Jude would sometimes stop her involuntary motions completely and assume a quiet, reflective manner that evoked a moment of pathos. It was the emergence of this heart-felt level of grief, unencumbered by indulgence in over-the-top rage, that made it possible for us to really work on her request to heal her heart. This process of transformation evolved amidst the fog of brain injury and crumbling whorl of degenerative disease.

Session Seven

The more we reminisced and grieved, the less Jude seemed to need to rage against her enemies. She leapt at the chance to tell me about her childhood when I reflected that she must have been especially resourceful to be able to keep her spirits up with all her recent, past, and present problems.

Jude modestly told me that, as a child, she was always watching out for other kids, and how keenly aware she was of the abusive conditions in the foster homes she was placed in after her own mother died from Huntington's disease. She described herself as someone who wouldn't stand for abuse, and constantly ran away to be with her older brother whom she related to as more of a "partner" than a brother. When Jude told this story she became a little girl with burning eyes and a great spirit.

Fortified with the spirit of independence and a sympathetic listener, Jude told me of how she was "put in the nut house" after her brain injury because "they" thought that she was crazy. She remembered watching television in the hospital and feeling "not there" when she tried to comprehend the images on the screen. These memories were difficult for her to hold without bringing up resentment toward those who unjustly labeled her as mentally impaired and used it to take her children away and gain control of her life. During this telling she managed to keep her anger in proportion and did not succumb to an uncontrollable fit of rage.

At the end of our session she was forthcoming with a spirited response to my comment on the incredible physical demands her Huntington's disease seemed to make on her. She said, with the steel and twinkle of the little foster child whose job it was to protect the world, *"It must be done!"* No messing around here. Jude was very serious about assuming an attitude of overcoming all her afflictions.

Session Eight

Jude's anger and resentment had now been bled off enough for her to entertain thoughts of making her own life better. We took this opportunity for setting goals to:

> find a new apartment or house.
> find a new doctor who would be more sympathetic to her needs.
> secure a reasonable income for survival
> fix her infected teeth and gums.
> and reestablish herself as a functional parent.

Leaving the task of list making, Jude spontaneously began to tell me about restoring old furniture with Rick Banks. Maybe the yearning to rebuild her life, made conscious through setting goals, triggered memories of rebuilding broken things.

Jude became almost giddy with this telling, and interspersed her story with singing her favorite songs. These songs were like mantras, that provided spiritual grounding through repetition, and usually consisted of old church hymns and catchy popular songs of the 1960s and 70s. "Jesus loves me this I know," "Kum bai ya," and the Beatles' "Hey Jude" were three of her favorites at this time.

I found myself singing along and sometimes waving my arms as if I shared her disease. Jude would cackle and hoot when she saw me getting animated. I became aware that singing and "dancing" with her was stretching the counseling skill of *matching* to a level almost beyond its intention, but found it a natural and powerful way for me to get into her mode.

We hooted and hollered away much of our session time, raucously singing her beloved songs and dancing around on the couch. I began to be aware that, for all her bitterness and anger, *Jude never sang angry or off color songs*. I experienced her songs as true reflections of the genuine decency and sweetness of her nature. They were indeed spiritual chants and served to ground her with their good feeling and familiarity.

The singing would inevitably be interrupted by Jude's request to light her fire. Being an ex-smoker I hate secondhand smoke, but endured it because I was in *her* home and smoking seemed one of her only real comforts. She never knew (and won't until she reads this account) that I carried extra sweatshirts in the trunk of my car to switch on the long drive home so I wouldn't reek of stale smoke.

Another tobacco-oriented ritual I endured was that of manufacturing countless cigarettes with a poorly engineered rolling machine. This task was unattainable for Jude because of her disability, and nearly impossible for me because of the impaired fine motor control of my left hand, and Jude's inadvertent crumpling of the tissue thin paper tubes when she handled the rolling kit while putting it away.

She laughed and encouraged me like a mother hen as I fumbled and tried to fit the fatally bent tubes into the carriage of the cheap little machine. "Yee Haw! Santa! Now you've got it!" she would cheer as I cranked out less than perfect product at a sluggish rate. I was deeply affected by her complete acceptance of my imperfection.

The power differential inherent in the counselor-client relationship was reversed when I manufactured cigarettes and Jude thrived in the nurturing role of being my coach and appreciative audience. Once again I was thankful to have found a *therapeutic activity that emerged from the natural flow of our relationship as two supportive friends.*

Session Nine

I always like to see historic photographs of my clients because reflections of their old self-image are often evident in captured moments from their pre-injury experiences. I also like to see pictures of pre-injury friends, family, surroundings, and possessions because these are real manifestations of *the world they created for themselves to live in.*

Photographs are not always readily available in a post-injury environment, because of the intense grieving they can easily evoke. Curiously Jude's photo albums were visible on a shelf that was within easy reach of the couch and not buried in her shrine. She did not object when I asked to see them, and let me take them down and go through them with her.

I saw her, in old environments, caring for children, joking with friends and family, and generally looking like she controlled, if not ruled her world like a queen bee. Evidence of her Huntington's disease was not obvious in the photographs, though pictures of her older brother, Wade, revealed gestures that indicated the progression of his own disease. Jude said she had small symptoms of her illness at the time some of the photographs were taken, but didn't dwell on it.

While we were looking at the pictures a vision of Jude as an older woman with a serene countenance and short gray hair popped into my mind. In this vision she exuded a deep sense of peace, and wisdom. I told her of my vision and tried to reflect it back to her as a potential reality.

She responded to my offering by telling me that she looked at her photo albums and cried and cried, mourning the loss of her family. Then she swiftly changed emotions and started cursing the judge, lawyer, doctor, ex-husband, and her brother. She promptly invoked retribution of her present enemies from the Hells Angels.

After her tirade, something snapped in me and I grasped, for a moment, how the Huntington's was *slurring* Jude's personality by randomly and involuntarily slinging her from one side of the emotional scale to the other. This was not the sort of emotional vacillation I often see in brain injury clients, and was an important insight into distinguishing the border between Jude's Huntington's disease and her brain injury.

I felt a need to ground the session after my epiphany and brought out a heart shaped beach stone that my wife had given me to offer to Jude as a present. Jude took it in her hands and held it close as if it were a real treasure. Then she told me to thank my wife and began to cry.

Her crying was interrupted by my big black dog who bounded in the open door from my car and licked Jude's salty face. Jude was delighted and overcome with joy at meeting the friendly animal. Sparked by the presence of the dog in her house, she ended the session by proclaiming that she wanted to bring her Huntington's stricken brother home from the hospital to live with her. In this moment of inspiration she stopped short, and wryly reflected "*I have to take care of everyone!*"

Session Ten

I make it a practice to let my clients read and approve the reports that I write about them. This makes me uncomfortable because, when I do so, I am sharing formally written objective observations and opinions about the very people who are the focus of my attempts to build immediate and intimate therapeutic relationships. Consequently I always preface the sharing of reports for approval with an apology to my clients for the experience they may have of feeling objectified by my writing *about* them.

Most clients don't quite comprehend what I am apologizing for and read the reports, or have me read them aloud, without complaint. Infrequently a client will have me rephrase an observation so that the insurance company doesn't get the "wrong idea" about them. Mostly their corrections, if any, consist of changing dates, spellings of names, or fixing my occasionally bad grammar. They sometimes tell me how well I have summed up their circumstances, which makes me feel even more uncomfortable because I fear they may be acquiescing to my "professional assessment" of their progress. I believe that it is essential, for the restoration of their self-confidence, that my clients feel on an equal enough basis with me to comfortably challenge my opinions and observations about them.

Jude listened to my stock apology and opted to read my last progress report for herself. She absorbed it with a keen interest and seemed expanded by the opportunity to see herself through my professional eyes. I did not sense any submission to my position in her life as a helping professional, and perceived her approval and comfort with the report to have come from a growing ability to see her situation with less distortion and more emotional control.

Her reading aroused my curiosity for I did not yet know the limits, if any, of her cognitive abilities and had not seen evidence of books, magazines, newspapers, or other literary material around her home. I was, however, aware that she was an avid fan of the Arts and Entertainment TV channel and that she enjoyed the intellectual stimulation of its varied programming. So, I figured she was pretty much on the ball.

After the study and acceptance of my report, Jude shifted to the more emotional ground of expressing her distress of feeling unsafe in the world. She told me about being raped as a child and how vulnerable she now felt when she ventured out at night. Then, she switched emotions and expressed anger at Sandy Morris for not protecting her. I acknowledged her feelings and listened to her rant against Sandy without questioning her logic in any way. Maybe she had identified Sandy as a protective mother figure, and her anger was actually aimed at her real mother who would or could not protect her as a child. This might also have explained her rage at Sandy for not safeguarding precious belongings during the recent move. In this light, Sandy's firing could be seen as a bid by Jude to take back control of her life as an adult.

Before I left, Jude made sure to ask me how my family was. She wanted a detailed report on everything that had happened in my life over the past week. I was encouraged that she did not forget this important ritual of connecting with me as a family friend, for it was essential to helping reestablish herself as someone who had her own family life and could afford to show interest in that of another.

Jude ended the session by expressing grief over how her Huntington's disease got in the way of her ability to live her life with ease. The direct expression of vulnerability and grief over her debilitating condition showed me that she was beginning to be able to separate and put boundaries around each of her multiple losses. I was very heartened by this progress because grieving her losses separately was much less overwhelming than experiencing them all lumped together as one.

Session Eleven

Arriving at Jude's apartment I was greeted by Mary, who introduced herself as a home care worker and had stayed longer than usual to finish some left over chores. Jude graciously invited me in and told me that Mary was her "friend" *not* her home care worker. Mary and Jude were in the midst of discussing the possibility of Jude's older disabled brother coming to live with Jude. This unrealistic plan included Mary's staying on as a live-in helper/nurse. Then Jude *and* Mary began to revile Jude's younger brother and conservator, John, for being out to grab the money from Jude's pending insurance award.

Mary seemed like a lively, supportive person who genuinely appreciated Jude's good nature. She also worried me a bit by reinforcing that some of Jude's more outlandish hopes, dreams and paranoid fantasies were grounded in reality. It occurred to me that Mary might be grooming Jude to feather her (Mary's) own bed as a future and indispensable caregiver. Unlike Mary, I felt it was best to simply acknowledge Jude's wacky takes on reality and showed a consistent lack of enthusiasm for any unrealistic and paranoid projections.

Today Jude was notably upset over a recent assault against her which occurred while she was out scrounging for cigarettes at three in the morning, after her landlord turned off the power and threw her out for playing loud music. She informed me that a man had offered her a cigarette in exchange for sexual favors. When she yelled "fuck you!" he grabbed at her breasts, frightening her. Luckily, she escaped without being assaulted further or having to use her hammer.

I wondered how her life would have been if she were provided with a home that was pleasant to spend the nights in—and an ample supply of cigarettes.

Jude and Mary were concerned that the neighbor upstairs was using a large crack in the ceiling as a peephole to spy on Jude. Though I had my doubts about the peeping Tom, I added the crack, which was really there, to my list of Jude's degrading living conditions.

The ease with which Mary encouraged Jude's paranoia made me wonder about her professionalism. Eventually Mary's employer caught wind of her unprofessional behavior, and she was removed, after some time, from her job as one of Jude's home care workers.

Jude protested Mary's impending removal but did not, at this time, decide to make a great issue of her future reinstatement. I wondered how adamantly the pre-injury Jude would have rushed to save a friend's job.

Session Twelve

Jude greeted me with her customary "Hi Angel Santa!," a big hug, and the usual inquiry of "How's your Angel family?" After I hugged her back and responded with a brief account of my family, we sat on the rickety furniture and she launched into grieving the death of Crazy Bill and how much she missed him. She repeatedly lamented how her heart "was broken" when he died and spent most of the rest of our session crying and mourning the loss of her lover.

Before it was time for me to leave, Jude looked up and asked to be driven to the local Salvation Army meeting hall, which she lovingly called the "Angel House." On our way out the door she motioned to her apartment and shouted, "I hate that place! Let me out!" When we passed a police car on the road she started telling me about a TV show she had recently seen on "cop killings" and how deeply she was affected while watching it.

In spite of her mistrust toward some of the institutions created to care for her, Jude kept a trusting and open relationship with the Salvation Army where she often went for aid and social contact. When I dropped her off at their building, she insisted that I come in to meet the director whom she counted as a friend. Surprisingly, she introduced me to this important person in her life not as "Santa," but as "Sol, my counselor." This choice of names stunned me because it showed that she was either able to choose the appropriate social response for specific situations, or that she wanted to impress her friend that she was undertaking her rehabilitation in a purposeful manner.

Maybe Jude wasn't as eccentric as I thought and was consciously using the privacy of our therapy to express her idiosyncrasies. If this were the case, I was gravely mistaken to conclude that her behavior in the therapy room was indicative of her behavior in the world.

Once again, I was slapped in the face with my own prejudice that if people look and act odd, they *are* odd. You'd think that I would have learned that this was not the case when I was poking around the world after my own brain injury, encountering people who treated me like I was not all there. I just didn't look like I was all there with half of my face drooping, but God Damn it! I was, and felt terrible about how people seemed to treat me as if I weren't.

31

I sometimes wondered if Jude felt at all self-conscious swaying around the world looking like a drunk, but never mustered the courage or heart to challenge her woman's vanity. I just assumed that she was too busy trying to control her erratic body to worry about how she looked to others. It would have been interesting to ask her.

My anguished misgivings about appearances were left for me to bear alone and Jude never let on if she knew that I was affected. She seemed truly one of the least pretentious people I have known and reserved her negative judgment only for those whom she perceived to have hurt her. My petty prejudice was not enough to put me on that list. Her generosity of spirit was one of her greatest attributes.

Session Thirteen

Jude was very excited and reported right away that she had seen her teenage son Bobby twice since our last session! I got the feeling that if nothing else happened in her world, this would be enough to sustain her for eternity. She was so excited by filling me in on the details of her visit with him that I wondered if we could dredge up anything else to talk about for the rest of the hour.

When we eventually got around to working on her losses, I brought up that I had recently spoken with her lawyer, Robin Gower, and found him to genuinely have her interests at heart. Jude immediately yelled "Asshole!," informed me that she didn't trust Robin, and proclaimed, "Then I will hire my *own* lawyer!" I perceived this response to come from a place of self-determination and told her that I thought it was a great idea, even though I personally disagreed with her assessment of Robin.

On this day my wife, Gloria, came with me and was waiting in the car, reading a book during my visit with Jude. I had been wanting Jude to meet my wife for some time and invited her to come outside with me to the car at the end of our session.

Jude was excited to meet a new person she had heard so much about, and greeted Gloria enthusiastically. She leaned in the car window and embraced Gloria with an open smile. Then she exclaimed, with great feeling, "Oh! You're *so* beautiful!" As Gloria warmly returned the embrace, I pondered Jude's remarkable exclamation with a curious heart. Was she comparing herself to Gloria? Was she grieving the loss of her own looks? *Or was she genuinely struck with Gloria's beauty and spontaneously expressing her feelings?*

By having Jude meet my family I hoped to deepen the opportunity for her to relate to me as a married friend. Now, every time she asked me about my "Angel family," she could have a real image of my wife to go with her question. Hopefully, through my association as a friend with a wife and family, Jude could work to reestablish an image of herself as a family person with functional friendships. As time passed she regularly began to expand her ritual questions about the health of my family with "How's your Angel wife?"

Before I drove off for the day, Jude caught me tracing the pattern of a geometric design that was carved on my belt buckle. When I sheepishly acknowledged my doodling, she quipped "That's okay. I guess you never drove in your own parking lot!" This site-specific joke showed me that she had increased her comfort level in relating to me with more sophisticated banter. At this level of relationship, Jude was able to lay aside her grief and begin to experience me as someone to play with.

Session Fourteen

During the past week I had occasion to consult with Jude's younger brother and legal guardian, John, about my work with his sister. John was extremely sympathetic with Jude's losses and did not seem at all the money grubbing "Asshole" she portrayed in her bitter tirades against him.

I got the feeling that being Jude's conservator was not a responsibility that John relished, and that he was doing it out of a sense of love and duty to his family. It also seemed to me that if John were able to express such tenderness and appreciation for his sister, she must have a tender place in her heart for him, no matter how tinged it was with bitterness and disappointment.

It did not take much to draw out Jude's feelings towards her younger brother. A question about their childhood together brought out the heart-rending story of how she and John were all the family that was left after their parents were gone and their older brothers put in foster homes. In those days she was *his* guardian, and "He was an angel." Now, "The Devil has him, and he (John) has taken my life away!" As usual, I simply acknowledged the loss and moved ahead asking if she had any pictures of him.

Jude rummaged around in the shrine and produced a photograph. I noted that this photograph was not with her albums, but hidden away, almost in exile (or protected), from the more accessible photographic memories of her pre-injury life with her other brothers and Crazy Bill. I was very impressed that she had relented enough to show me John's picture.

The photograph revealed a pleasant looking young man who bore a strong family resemblance to Jude. While I took off my glasses and carefully studied John's image, Jude leaned on my shoulder and brought her face close in to mine. Her Huntington's movements stopped and she grew wistful and very soft. Then she started to talk: Telling sweet stories about her childhood that included memories of family camping trips, playing "bang bang guns" with John, romping with her big golden "Woofie dog Buster," and acting her role in Cowboys and Indians as "Little Bear." Jude radiated contentment when she told me these stories and readily acknowledged the fact that her childhood with John was built on a foundation of mutual affection and love.

It was my hope that we would discover other such openings into Jude's positive feelings for her brother. I believed that the more she was able to *feel* as she did before her injuries, the better she would be able to fully grieve her losses without being overcome by their negative effects on her life.

Session Fifteen

Jude had just come home from the city where she had undergone a battery of neuropsychological examinations to help determine the degree of injury to her brain that was caused by her accident. Neuropsychological examinations are not always a pleasant experience because they are designed to ferret out cognitive disability and do so by challenging clients' abilities. Therefore they are often difficult, exhausting, and demand long periods of concentrated effort. These hardships can be mitigated by sensitive and compassionate administration of the examination. Jude did not experience her examiner as sympathetic or compassionate. She told me that "They (the test givers) abused me!" and "took my toys (some of the test materials) away before I was done!" This simply could have been her frustrated response to being cut off by a time limit before she had finished a particular test. For either or both of these reasons the tests proved a very negative event for her.

Fortunately, Jude's experience of being tested was not the only memory of her trip. She did get to meet an old friend, who ran a small used clothing shop, and was given some new (old) clothes. Jude told me that she and her friend cried, hugged, and carried on like "real girlfriends" for the short time that they were together. After sharing her story, she went into another room to change and came back to model her new dress and belt. She looked great.

Jude was very easy to draw out after her modeling session and informed me that her friends and family used to call her "Mama" and "Auntie" because she took care of everyone. I made a note to myself that these nicknames would evoke an image of herself as an authoritative and supportive person in her community of family and friends. This was someone she had surely been before her recent losses. It was not a great leap from Jude's recognition of who she had been before her accident, to the expression of anger about having lost her status in her old life.

This anger found its usual channel in an outburst about how she "got screwed" and how "they took my life away!" She swore at the judge who took her kids from her, and told me that she was going to "march into his office and dump a bag of dog shit on his desk!" Then she proceeded to tell me that the Hells Angels were going to "camp out on his lawn."

After she bled off some anger, Jude assured me that she did not swear around her children and told me that she "knew who to swear around." This was another indication that she was beginning to redevelop an image of herself that included a sense of propriety and awareness of how she was perceived by others.

Session Sixteen

Last week during our visit, while I was looking around in the shrine to take out some photographs of Jude's children, I accidentally dropped a small metal hairpin behind the refrigerator. This pin happened to have been given to Jude by one of her kids and had great sentimental value. It was so small and insignificant to me that I didn't remember seeing it when I very carefully removed the photographs to look more closely at them. However, it was extremely significant and important *to Jude* who informed me that she cried about the hairpin's loss until her son Bobby came over and promised to find it for her.

Bobby couldn't find the pin in the collection of odds and ends that had fallen behind the refrigerator and left his mother in tears until he promised to return and find it. The hairpin was still missing and I was concerned that Jude might find me guilty of violating the sanctity of her shrine and fire me as she had Sandy.

Feeling responsible for the disappearance of the pin, I dove behind the refrigerator and carefully looked for it. I really didn't know if it had ever been on top of the appliance, and didn't have much faith in its turning up in the rubble between the refrigerator and the wall.

Jude hopefully watched me search and did not display the agitation that I feared. She actually expressed more sadness than anger at the loss, and laid absolutely *no* blame on me. I was relieved that she had not been triggered into rage by the innocent circumstances of this loss, and noted it as evidence of the solid nature of our rapport.

The disparity between Jude's excellent progress in counseling, and the deteriorating state of her health and living conditions concerned me greatly. It also showed the futility of her ability, under the present circumstances, to change her world from the inside out. *The fact that she was rapidly rediscovering herself as a positive and functional person seemed to have little or no effect upon the speed with which the system, set up to care for her, was able to meet her fundamental needs of adequate housing and health care.*

This situation spurred me to advocate more vigorously for what I perceived were vital needs in Jude's life. I also worried that she might adopt an attitude of defeat when she realized that her efforts to change herself positively did not necessarily correlate to positive change in the quality of her life.

Now that we had begun to uncover her positive nature and reinforce her self-image as a fighter, there seemed no stopping Jude in her drive to become whole and healthy again. She was very happy and ready to meet with Dr. Keller, a genetic specialist from Victoria, to see about starting a new treatment for her Huntington's disease.

Session Seventeen

Jude reluctantly gave me permission to fax my reports to her brother, John, so that he could be kept up to date on her progress. As we talked about John she grew very angry and began swearing, referring to him as "The Fucker!" I let this go by without reminding her of how tenderly she had recently spoken of him.

While I was struggling to roll a cigarette with the impossible machine, Jude quietly studied me and quipped "Will ya look at the concentration, eh?" This comment elicited laughter on both our parts and could have reminded her of the manner she used to relate to her younger brother when she taught him to do things many years ago. It also gave her the opportunity, at my expense, to reclaim her position in the family as the older and more accomplished sibling. The changing dynamics in our relationship always seemed to provide a stage for her to work on important issues in her life.

Before I left, Jude told me how excited she was about the up coming meeting with Dr. Keller and chanted over and over "It's a blessing…It's a blessing…It's my turn now!…It's my turn now…" The meeting was scheduled for six days from today's session and Jude wanted me to be there.

Session Eighteen
(Visit with Dr. Keller)

During Jude's consultation with Dr. Keller, he asked her what she wanted most from treatment. She answered, without pause, "To help my dancing." Dr. Keller offered treatment through medication on a three-week trial basis. He warned that initial dosage required a process of "balancing" to obtain the optimum effect of controlling Jude's symptoms. I was worried about debilitating side effects and voiced my concern. Like most doctors, Dr. Keller assured me that side effects should be easily manageable and most likely non-existent. He was right.

Dr. Keller went on to underscore the importance of strengthening Jude's general level of health through *the elimination of her oral abscesses (through removal of her teeth)* and addressing the problems of her weight loss and lack of sleep. Dr. Keller's forthright prescription for a dramatic improvement in Jude's basic health needs encouraged me to advocate harder for more timely attention to her dental needs, improved medical support, and better living conditions.

I was gratified to see that Dr. Keller had put a rather high priority on getting Jude's teeth attended to for I perceived them as her most serious and pressing medical problem. The abscesses in her mouth were so extreme that she was in constant pain and taking more and more painkillers to make it through the day. I was amazed that she was able to carry on at all under the torturous conditions of her infected gums.

Sometimes, when I saw her, her jaw would be so swollen and bulged out with infection that she would hardly be able to speak, much less concentrate on the work of counseling for all the pain killers she was taking. Obviously this was a critical problem and I was appalled that it was not being immediately and effectively addressed by her support systems. Jude blamed her doctors, Sandy, and her accident for her dental problems. After studying the situation, I came to the conclusion that she had assessed it rather accurately.

At one point Jude's doctors had prescribed medication to treat heart symptoms that she manifested in hospital after her head injury. It occurred to me that these symptoms might have been psychosomatic indications of the state of her "broken heart" after losing her family, and not necessarily deserving of treatment by medication commonly used for physical heart problems.

One of the side effects of this medication is that it greatly reduces the production of saliva. Saliva is a natural antibiotic and must be present in the mouth to help, along with the activity of oral hygiene, keep it infection free. Jude ceased to brush her teeth altogether after her injury because she "just didn't care" and had an increasingly difficult time managing a toothbrush with her rapidly advancing movement disorder.

She expected Sandy, her support worker, to buy a toothbrush and brush her teeth for her. Sandy could not perform this chore because it was not practical, part of her training, nor in her job description. For these reasons she came to bare all the blame for Jude's rotting mouth.

It did not take a dental rocket scientist to figure out how to best deal with this situation. The obvious plan of choice was to have Jude's rotten teeth pulled, her infections treated, and a new set of false teeth made and fitted to her mouth. This did not prove as simple as it might have seemed.

First of all, Jude did not want to have her teeth pulled and get dentures. She desperately wanted to keep as many of her own teeth as possible and have the dentist reconstruct her mouth attaching new sections of false teeth to remaining solid natural structure. The problem was that, after examination, there proved to be not enough solid natural structure left to attach prostheses to. We went round and round trying to convince Jude that the days of flashing her "natural" smile were over and the best choice was to let the dentists replace her teeth.

I am sure that it was nothing we said that finally convinced Jude to go ahead and have her teeth pulled. She eventually had to accept the fact that she couldn't go on living with the constant pain and infection of her rotting gums and teeth. Her surrender to the inevitable took several months, after which time all the appointments that were made for dental surgery had to be canceled and postponed indefinitely. This frustrating state of affairs was because Jude's brother and conservator, John, wasn't answering his phone or responding to messages for weeks on end.

The question arose in my mind, why such high-priority medical treatment, that was supported by all professionals involved, had to wait for non-forthcoming permission. It seemed to me that the system of conservatorship that was set up to ensure Jude's safety was putting her at more risk in its attempts to "protect her from herself."

Session Nineteen

During our session Jude stumbled on some of the shrine that was spilling over onto the floor. She immediately cursed both the apartment and her Huntington's disease. I reminded her of our recent visit with Doctor Keller and why we were trying to knock down the symptoms of her disease. I suppose I really didn't have to remind Jude why it was desirable to treat her disease. She knew better that anyone how difficult it was to live with its debilitating symptoms.

I never knew what a session would bring and not long after Jude stumbled, I bore witness to an unexpected display of raw emotion as a fire engine roared by the apartment with its loud siren and blazing lights. Upon hearing the siren, Jude immediately became paralyzed with fear. Her eyes grew round and she threw herself on the couch and curled up into a ball.

I put my arms around her and quieted her down with a gentle soothing voice telling her that she was safe with me, inside her home. I recognized her response to the siren as a symptom of post-traumatic stress directly related to her accident.

If we have no story for our trauma, we are compelled to *re-live* its stress, when triggered, through our body—the only means of recall we have available. On the other hand, if we have a story, we can attribute a triggering occurrence to the story and bypass the body's natural compulsion to re-live the stress of the trauma. With this in mind, I asked Jude, after she calmed down, if she wanted to learn how to hear sirens without being overwhelmed by uncontrollable terror. She said that she would like to, so I began to help her solidify a story for her accident.

Jude bravely undertook to tell me what she remembered of being struck down. She described being "hit like a shotgun!," "hurt all over!"—"The car that hit me was going a hundred miles an hour!" Then she told me about the man who came to her aid; "tall, with dark hair—he brought me a woolly blanket." She remembered a *fire engine* rather than an ambulance because "no ambulances could come that night."

I helped her confirm to herself that the next time she would hear a siren she might be *reminded of the fire engine that came to help her the night she got hit*. This thought calmed her down and she seemed to transform her terror into compassion by saying, "I pray to God the people in the accident (that today's fire engine

44

was going to) are okay!" She also added that squealing tires scared her by *reminding* her of the night of her accident, and went on to tell me that the man who hit her "went home to hide at his mother's." I didn't know how she knew this, and simply acknowledged her outburst of anger when she went on to threaten him, and his mother, with a visit from the Hells Angels. Jude ended her talk about the man who hit her by jesting, "I guess his job is to get drunk and drive around and hit people on sidewalks!"

I was struck by the chasm between Jude's ability to respond as in terror to her buried trauma and make a joke about the person who caused it. It was my hope that the opening we explored into the core of her ordeal might lead, along with more therapy, to the establishment of a viable story for her trauma.

Session Twenty

Jude's focus was anger. Her recent birthday of November 17 reminded her of her brother John's which is next door at November 16. This got her thinking about John and how he "put me in the nut house" and "took away my life and money." She was spitting mad about this and started squawking "fuck! fuck! fuck! fuck!" like an angry bird. Then, in a flash of insight she fixed me with her gaze and said "John *wanted* me to be angry, so he could put me in the nut house!" I then asked her if she was going to let her brother control her like that? She paused, looked at me again, and went on to tell me about how her grandmother got "ripped off" and how "it's in the family!"

At this point in our conversation, her landlord pounded on the door to tell her to clean up the junk outside of her front door. Jude flew into a rage and accused him of throwing away her pumpkin, which was left over from Halloween and rotting outside. After the landlord left, Jude fumed about how she had no control over her own home and was at the mercy of the "Asshole landlord."

Session Twenty-One

A while ago I had asked Mary to leave the apartment when I was counseling Jude because of the distraction. Mary seemed to have no problem with my request and usually left us alone while she went out to do errands. This arrangement was *not* okay with Jude and she began our visit by chastising me for not allowing Mary to be present at our sessions. Jude felt she should be able to invite whomever she wished to be in *her* home. In this case she was insisting on having a bit of a party with two of her favorite people. Though I welcomed this as an expression of Jude's self-determination, I felt the need to claim a special relationship as her counselor. In doing so I wanted to ensure an environment, without distractions, where more progress in therapy could be made.

Jude was particularly sharp and admitted during the course of bantering with me that she was a "bullshitter." When I asked her if that meant I could be a "bullshitter" too, she replied that I could *not* because I was a counselor. She then told me that counselors had the responsibility to "tell the truth—no bullshit!" followed by the lament that her "heart was still broken." I asked her if she was "bullshitting" me about that and she said "No."

In order to give her more opportunity to call her own shots, I offered to reduce the frequency of my visits from once a week to every two weeks (with Mary present sometimes, if necessary, to sweeten the deal). Jude did not like the sound of this offer and asked me to continue coming every week.

At the end of our session she asked me how I slept at night. I said that I usually slept well and she launched into complaints about her lack of restful sleep. After I brought it to her attention, she would not acknowledge that smoking cigarettes and drinking cup after cup of coffee at night might be contributing to her insomnia.

Session Twenty-Two

When Jude asked me about my family I told her that a black bear swam over to the island I lived on and was raiding the hives of local beekeepers. Instead of showing concern for the safety of my community, or growling like a bear which she sometimes did to show her affinity with its tenacious spirit, she softly sang in a shy little voice, "Isn't it funny how bears love honey!" This response, though appropriate, seemed less spunky than usual and I wondered what had happened, since our last visit, to cause such passive childlike behavior.

I did not have to wait long to find out, for Mary, who was wrapping up to leave, took me aside to warn me about a woman named Karen. Karen had parked her camper van in the driveway next to the apartment and was using Jude's kitchen and bathroom facilities. Mary was upset because she felt that Karen had "moved in and taken over" Jude's life. Karen was not home, but would have to return because she kept a disabled daughter, who couldn't go out with her, housed in the van. It sounded like Karen had taken advantage of Jude's boundless generosity and was moving in for some sort of kill. Like a fool, I didn't put my guard up.

Another indication that Jude was different was that, for the first time since I had known her, she expressed distrust of me and Paul. She called us "bad boys" and referred to previous male workers and professional helpers as "good boys." Then she began to screech "fuck fuck fuck fuck." I tried to quiet her down by telling her that we only used the "fuck fuck" routine when she needed to boil off anger to "get back to herself." She looked at me defiantly and said "But I've always been myself!" I couldn't really refute this point and was impressed by her defiance. It was almost as if someone had turned her against me.

I told her that she had nothing to fear from me and that, as far as I was concerned, she was the "boss" of her own therapy program. She loved it when I called her the "boss" and said that she wanted to keep seeing me "no matter what *they* say." Who were "they," and what had "they" said?

Session Twenty-Three

Jude puttered around straightening up her apartment. She was delighted when I reflected out loud, "Jude runs her home!" and she continued to fuss and show me new bits and pieces of the shrine in a calm and orderly fashion. Altogether she was relatively peaceful, swearing somewhat freely, but showing no overt anger until she started to talk about Karen.

Karen had been criticizing Jude for keeping a messy house and smoking too much. Jude complained bitterly that it was Karen who was responsible for messing up the house, and then had the nerve to act in a bossy manner. This was an indication that the honeymoon was over and I wondered if Karen would ever be around when I visited. She sure seemed to keep her distance.

Near the end of our session Karen did indeed show up and walked right in to the apartment like she owned the place. Jude introduced me as "Santa." I immediately corrected her and told Karen that my name was "Sol" and that I was a counselor employed by Jude's insurance company. Karen was surprisingly meek and left after a couple of minutes.

After Karen left, I asked Jude about her "Angels" and how she saw herself in relation to them. She replied that her "Angels" were her children and that she was the "Mama Angel." I was encouraged to see her maintain her identity as the head of her household—even if it was not all under her roof.

Jude also expressed her frustration over things not getting done in her life. Her complaints were all related to regaining her health and autonomy. She stated her demands to include getting her teeth fixed, finding a new apartment or house, and establishing a reliable source of income to provide adequate money for food and cigarettes. This list of wants was a welcome change from the litany of retribution that she used to demand against those she felt responsible for her losses.

Session Twenty-Four

Since my last visit, Jude saw her lawyer, Robin Gower, with Paul and was proud of herself for taking some responsibility for her own life. She was adamant about having the right to choose her own lawyer and defiantly stated, "There's nothing wrong with me!" I told her that I agreed that there was nothing "wrong" with her at all, only that she had suffered injuries that might be causing her some sadness and trouble. She admitted this was probably so, but was not so injured that "they" had the right to take her kids away. Again I agreed and said that I thought it was unjust for anyone to take advantage of her injured state in order to remove her children from her when she was incapable of advocating for herself.

Then I gave her a small picture of an Angel that my wife had drawn. It bore an uncanny resemblance to Jude and she promptly named it "Mamma Angel." The picture, in a gold frame, was immediately hung on the wall and served the three-fold therapeutic purpose of showing my regard for her, providing a healthy reflection of her self-image, and connecting her family to mine. The fact that part of my world was now installed in hers reinforced her role as a functional and mutually respected family friend.

Jude was extremely angry with Karen for a remarkable and disturbing reason. This was because Karen had told the director of the Salvation Army that I had been sexually inappropriate during a counseling session by describing how I made love to my wife. This had no basis in truth, and was a totally fabricated assault on my professionalism. Jude was livid that Karen would lie about me in a way that could hurt me. My strange feelings from two weeks ago about Jude's being turned against Paul and me by some unknown source were validated and I determined to apprise my employer of Karen's false allegations against me. Upon doing so I discovered that I was not the only professional helper that Karen had been trying to discredit with lies so that she could isolate Jude for her own exploitive purposes.

As it turned out Karen was known, to both the Salvation Army and my employer, as a local troublemaker and her accusations against me were dismissed as those of a harmful and unreliable source. Not long after her exposure as an unwelcome person in Jude's life, Karen disappeared from the area leaving behind only an old pair of hiking boots and the then unknown suggestion to another "friend" to seek out Jude's hospitality.

Jude confirmed that she wanted to continue counseling until her "heart was fixed." This was a tall order for she would most likely complain of a broken heart until she regained care of her children. I told her that I could not guarantee her children returning to her home, but did foresee a time when she would be able to have a full relationship with them again.

Session Twenty-Five

Since I had not seen Jude over Christmas, I wondered how she had fared without me. I was glad to find her more centered than usual and assumed that her improved condition was the result of increased contact with her children over the holiday period.

Jude mentioned again how glad she was to have got rid of Karen and reiterated how her heart was still broken and how much she wanted her children back. I could only simply acknowledge these feelings as irrefutable facts, and assured her that I would remain seeing her as a counselor until she felt her heart was healed.

It was important to begin weaning Jude from counseling long before the end of our counseling relationship, so I offered her a reduction in the frequency of my visits from four to three times a month and she said she was willing to see how it worked out. She accepted this plan without any indication of distress.

Giving her control of her recovery involved listening very carefully and remaining flexible in my response to her expressed need for counseling.

Session Twenty-Six

I came in with a cold and began to complain about my aches and pains. Jude turned to Mary, who was finishing up to leave the house, and said, referring to me in a playful manner, "Poor baby's whining!—just like a man!"

After Mary left, Jude got looser with her language and started to mumble "fuck fuck fuck fuck." Then she grinned at me, said "Fuck fixes the heart!" and teased me stating, "I never swore before I met you!" I answered, "Once we're wounded, it takes a long time to heal." Jude grew thoughtful and mused, "Just like eagles, we crash and burn!" This statement gave me an indication that she was ceasing to see herself as a victim, and beginning to identify with symbols of strength and power—even though she was describing them during their down time.

Jude ended our session by telling me that she wanted to go with Paul to visit the judge who took her kids away and ask for them back. She didn't mention anything about dumping dog droppings on his desk, so I encouraged her to "be nice and polite." This almost got by her, but she grinned wickedly at me and said "You *gotta* be kidding!"

Session Twenty-Seven

Jude received her first prescription of Dr. Keller's Huntington's medication today and was very excited and ready to start taking her doses, which were to be administered by her home care workers under the direction of a public nurse. The nurse, who was there to train Mary, mentioned a problem about needing some kind of "legal permission" for the home care workers to be able to administer the drug. I groaned inside, thinking that Jude's hard won progress in treating her disease had come up against yet another bureaucratic hurdle.

After I introduced myself and voiced my frustration, the nurse assured me that she would vigorously pursue a solution to the problem and there would be almost no interruption in treatment. She proved as good as her word and called me at home in the evening to say that she had wrangled the official go-ahead to give Jude her medication.

Oblivious to the complications around her treatment, Jude managed to provide coffee and treats despite the fact that her cheeks were blown up the size of tennis balls with abscesses, and she was gulping Tylenol #2's for the pain.

After some fuss, she was willing to let me miss next week's session because I was serious about beginning to wean her from my services. For the first time ever, she told me that her "heart was better." I was gratified to hear this but was on guard that she might be telling me what she thought I wanted to hear. Suspicion aside, I took serious note of this reversal and started to tally the times she acknowledged her heart healing against those when she despaired of its being broken. It was wonderful working with Jude because she was always so forthcoming about the immediate state of her being.

Session Twenty-Eight

Except for the recent holiday season, this was the first time that I had not seen Jude on a weekly basis. It was, in fact, our first attempt at seeing each other on my newly proposed reduced schedule. I was curious to discover if the change in rhythm had affected our progress. This change in schedule went unnoticed and Jude did not mention that she missed last week's session. I remarked how smooth the transition to our new schedule felt and discussed the possibility of seeing her five weeks in a row, then skipping two, for a while—eventually reducing to every two weeks. I determined that she would hardly notice the reduction at this rate. I asked Jude if she had experienced any changes in her Huntington's symptoms over the past two weeks since she began taking her new medication. She replied that she was feeling some relief but did not go into detail.

Jude's teeth were giving her a lot of trouble and she reported that she had upped her pain medication from Tylenol #2's to #3's (with codeine). This was very disturbing. While the lawyers and bureaucrats were spinning their wheels, my client's health was rapidly deteriorating.

Along with her physical complaints, Jude was furious at the company that provided her with home care workers because they were finally getting around to having Mary removed from her case. She said she was particularly upset because she and Mary were becoming "attached to each other." I was interested in Jude's choice of language to describe her growing relationship with Mary, because it indicated that she was capable of seeing herself intimately relating with another person outside of her family and me.

At the end of the session Jude astonished me by matter-of-factly stating that she had a boyfriend, named Philip, who had moved in with her. If this were true, it was the first that I had heard of it.

Session Twenty-Nine

As I entered Jude's apartment I almost stumbled over a pair of large dirty work boots. I asked Jude who they belonged to, and she said they were Philip's. When I inquired more about Philip, she told me that he was a friend of Karen's who was working in town and needed a place to stay for the duration of his job.

Jude carefully explained that Philip slept in her bedroom and she slept on the couch. Giving Philip a place to stay, even if it was in her grubby little apartment, was yet another indication of her graciousness. Even though Jude had next to nothing herself, she was happy to be able to share it with another.

I worried a bit that Philip, who was not at home when I was there, might be taking advantage of Jude's good nature by using her home as a crash pad. I was also concerned about the potential for him to sexually exploit her, and determined to check out the situation with Paul and the other professionals involved in her case.

Jude quickly put the subject of Philip aside and informed me that she had recently seen her doctor, who was getting her more medication for Huntington's disease since she had used up her trial dosage. She added that she liked how the medication was reducing her symptoms, and stated appreciation for what her doctors were doing for her. This was a far cry from the bitterness she had expressed toward her doctors when I first met her.

As quickly as she had left the subject of Philip, Jude switched to telling me about the experience of her accident. She said that she thought she was being "shot" when she was hit. I asked her why "shot," and by whom? She did not answer my questions but brought forth what she called her "accident shirt" which she was wearing when she was struck down. This was a stained and crumpled long sleeved cotton pullover that she easily extricated from its special place in her shrine. She knew exactly where it was and told me that she kept the shirt to help her "remember" her accident. It seemed she had been consciously working on the task we set to remember her accident. I was also impressed that she was able to talk about her experience so dispassionately while holding a "memory" of it in her hands.

Next Jude jumped to talking about her children as if she were still actively involved in their lives. She talked with the animation of a loving mother and excitedly reported another visit from her son, Bobby. Bobby had been sneaking away from Brent and Mara's home to visit his mother. Jude loved it that Bobby was breaking orders to visit her and went on to tell me about the time she got caught "smoking in the girls' room" in high school.

She showed real delight in recounting how Bobby had recently been caught smoking in the boy's room at school: "—Just like me!…Well almost, because it was the *girls'* room for me and the *boys'* room for Bobby!" Jude got a real kick out of how neatly the gender switch from girls' to boys' room accented the telling of her story.

Talking fondly of Bobby, and the difficulties she had being with him, prompted Jude to start ranting against Brent and the judge that gave her children to him. This rant, though charged with anger and indignation, was expressed more like a litany than an overpowering emotional storm and showed me, once again, that Jude was gaining control over her emotions.

After burning off some anger at Brent and the judge, Jude launched into a story about a "Harley movie" she had recently seen on TV. She was especially impressed with the portrayal of the Harley-riding "cop and his wife."—another link to the reminiscence of her and Crazy Bill on their motorcycle.

Session Thirty

When I arrived at Jude's, the door was answered by a tall blonde man who introduced himself as Philip. He was clean and respectful and did not immediately strike me as a threatening presence in Jude's life. He told me, when I asked, that he would be staying at the apartment for another few weeks until his job in town was over. He showed an interest in counseling but I informed him that it was a private business between Jude and me and he left saying that he wouldn't be at the apartment, in the future, on the days that I came to see Jude.

Jude, for her part, did not complain and seemed content to carry on without Philip in the room. I mentioned Philip's presence in Jude's life to Paul and he was not particularly concerned about her safety, so I decided to keep a watch on the situation and take my cues from Jude if anything seemed to become threatening.

On this day Jude's abscesses were especially troublesome. Both her cheeks were ballooned with infection. It was a wonder that she was up and around at all—much less willing to talk with me. She reported that Paul had taken her to the doctor's for more painkillers.

Jude was more positively oriented than I could imagine under her painful circumstances and told me, once again, how well she liked the drugs Dr. Keller had given her. She reported that her Huntington's movements were less out of control and it seemed easier to perform voluntary actions. She also said she felt generally calmer and more self-contained.

Despite the great pain of her abscesses, Jude's yearning to have her family back together remained at the forefront of her distress. Accordingly, in the midst of talking about her various problems, she repeated over and over "*I sure miss my Angel kids.*" My response to this constant lament was "I know, sweetheart, I know." I believed that simply giving Jude the opportunity to voice her greatest loss, *over and over*—and be heard, *over and over*, was the best therapy I, or anyone else, could provide for a mother who had lost the right to be with her children. The more Jude had the opportunity to simply express her grief, the less angry she became—and the sadder and more fully she was able to grieve. In spite of her great sorrow, Jude had somehow found the energy to collect some Valentines

Day treats for Jamie. She was very proud of her efforts and showed me a plate of red sparkled heart shaped cookies she was saving to give him the next time he visited her. After showing me the cookies, Jude expressed her anger at the judge, her brother John, and Sandy. Then she told me about the night Crazy Bill died, his funeral, and, for the first time, his parents' grief.

She later went into some detail about how she felt used by Sandy's making money off her disability "like it was an industry." I was impressed with Jude's ability to see herself objectified in such a manner, but couldn't really know all of Sandy's motives for being a caregiver. I did, however, from my knowledge of Sandy, not really believe that she was exclusively motivated by financial gain.

Jude's statement about Sandy gave me pause to explore my own motives for being a counselor. Though I had on occasion privately commented to my wife that Jude's needs created "quite an industry for caregivers," I perceived the support of her rehabilitation as a reflection of the value Canadian society places on the maintenance of its members in health and dignity. I am grateful that this national inclination has allowed me to contribute meaningfully to Jude's recovery.

Jude's progress showed up in my notes with the repeated weekly observation that she was *"becoming more solid."* The positive momentum of the reestablishment of herself as a whole person, with a healing heart, was becoming strong enough to carry her through the difficulties inherent in her struggle to gain support from a balky but well-meaning system.

Session Thirty-One

Once again Jude reported favorably on the symptomatic relief provided by Dr. Keller's medication. It seemed to me that a haze had lifted from her, and that her face stopped twitching and was more in synch with her usually bright eyes. She also seemed more grounded.

As focused as she was, Jude chose to express more anger at the judge and welfare department, whom she perceived to have jointly taken her children from her. I was pleased to note, once again, the circumspect boundaries around her anger, and that she was able to be angry without letting it overwhelm her.

After she grieved the loss of her children, Jude assumed a playful attitude and teased me, saying that she wanted me to save *my* dog's poop for the bag she was collecting to dump on the judge's desk. I took the risk of calling her bluff, called her "chicken," and dared her to go to the judge's office and do the deed. As far as I know she never did.

Session Thirty-Two

Jude started off our session by telling me how much she missed her Angel kids and asking me what was new in my life. I acknowledged her loss and told her a bit about what was new with my wife and me. She responded by letting me know that she missed having someone to care for her like my wife cared for me.

She specifically referred to how much she missed having someone to fix her "ow-ees." She was very clingy, constantly rubbing my belly and touching my arm. Then she told me a recent vision about being raped.

Jude's vision was probably brought about by an experience during the past week involving a local taxi driver. This driver had circled her apartment building in his cab calling out that he would pay her twenty dollars to "suck his cock." Jude told him to "fuck off!" but he continued to circle the building squealing his tires. The noise of squealing tires deeply frightened Jude because it reminded her of her accident and previously abusive situations.

I encouraged her to go to the police, if she could identify the taxi driver, and told her that I was going to ask Paul to accompany her to the station. Jude then played the incident down, and told me to "just forget it!" as if she had no confidence in the system to protect her. I repeated that I was going to ask Paul to take her in to the police station to report the incident anyway, and she didn't object.

Other than report to responsible parties what I perceive as a dangerous situation, I do not feel that it is my duty to personally ensure my clients' safety. It was, however, my responsibility to help Jude modulate her emotions enough to ask a system she distrusted and hated for help if she felt she needed it. To this end I worked with her to create a "hate list" so that she could see how her anger and mistrust was distributed.

The list was as follows (not in order of intensity of hatred):

Sandy—"for ruining my teeth and losing my things"
Ex-husband Brent—"for taking away my children"
The cab driver—"for being a pervert"
The judge—"for taking away my children"
Younger brother John—"for taking away my life"

Welfare Department—"for taking away my children and not giving me enough to live on"

The landlord—"for being mean and kicking me out"

The hit and run driver—"for hitting me and giving me my brain injury"

Karen—"for bossing me around and messing up my place"

Lawyer Robin Gower—"for not getting me money or helping me get my kids back"

The man who first raped me—"for ruining my life"

Dr. Larsen (general practitioner)—"for taking away my life by signing my commitment order"

Jude's ability to list the people she "hated" without an uncontrollable display of extreme emotion showed me that much of her bitterness had burned off. I wrote down the hate list on my note pad and showed it back to her. Curiously, the police, as authority figures, were not on it. In fact she seemed to have an affinity for cops and identified with them as protectors who rode Harleys. Her identification with the police, in this manner, also gave an indication that some of her self-image was *still intact as a protector rather than a victim.*

Session Thirty-Three

When I came in Jude was watching a Willie Nelson special on TV and wanted to leave it on while I was there because she was enjoying it so much. She agreed to keep the volume low enough so that we could talk over it and was happy when I said that she could turn it up if a song came on that she particularly liked.

An important aspect of my practice as a rehabilitation counselor is that I choose, if possible, to see clients in their homes or places of their choice rather than in a professional counseling office. I believe that the work of reestablishing self-image is better done in environments where *they* can most easily visualize themselves living effectively. This even held true in Jude's case, in spite of her degrading living conditions, because it was her *home* and contained all the available remnants of her world. A familiar or inspirational environment can often provide rich material for the rebuilding of a shattered life.

Noticing Jude's keen interest in Willie Nelson prompted me to ask her where her attraction to country/folk music came from. I knew that she liked to make music because she was always singing the by now familiar assortment of tunes and hymns that I called her "personal healing mantras."

Jude warmed to this question and launched into telling me about her family band. She related that when she was younger, she was in a small country band with her two older brothers, Wade and Gordie, both of whom later became afflicted with Huntington's disease. Jude said she played guitar, fiddle, blues harp (harmonica), and sang. She was very proud that her little band had played a couple of gigs and really lit up when she told me of her musical history. Then she said how excited she was that her son Bobby had just acquired an electric guitar.

The wonderful thing about person centered therapy, as presented by Rogers, is that, if allowed, *the client can lead* a session into particular realms of reminiscence that better support and strengthen natural healing processes. Letting Jude keep Willie Nelson in view, while we talked, gave her, and me, the opportunity to tell the right stories and ask the right questions. Jude was very relaxed and more solid after sharing the story of her musical career.

We leaned back on the couch and she dropped some ashes on the filthy rug. I said jokingly, "Look at you! You just sit here and make your rug dirty!" Rather than be offended, Jude quipped "It's a hard job and someone's got to do it!"

Jude's good mood, enhanced by her musical memories, prompted her to report, again, how grateful she was for Dr. Keller's drugs. She pointed out, several times, that her eyes had stopped winking. I leaned over and took a look. Indeed, the winking had stopped! The two bright stars of her eyes shone back through the night sky of her unconscious grimaces.

She went on to tell me that she had a new home care worker, who had little experience with Huntington's Disease. This worker asked Jude if she were drunk. She was surprised at the question and looked at me in amazement.

This started me thinking about Jude's awareness of herself in the world. If Jude had suffered only a brain injury, I might have assumed that this particular lack of self-awareness was related to her loss of self-image. However, I was compelled to further question the nature of her perception of herself due to the additional presence of the Huntington's disease. Had she already gone through the process of conforming her image of herself to the physical characteristics of her disease *before* her brain injury? In exploring this question I had to remind myself that she grew up in a Huntington's family and the unusual movements associated with the disease might not have seemed all that unusual to her. Since Jude's loss of self-image more often seemed centered around her role as a mother, housekeeper and independent person, and *not* around her presentation as a disabled person, I decided to concentrate my energy on helping her reestablish herself in those former roles. Jude often reminded me that *her brain injury marked the point when her life changed for the worse.* Her picture of herself, as a person with Huntington's disease, seemed comparatively well integrated into her self-image and was mostly outside the scope of my work with her.

Though I must have appeared long lost in thought pondering the implications of her dual disabilities, Jude did not seem to notice. She interrupted my reverie by telling me how much she liked her new homemaker, because she made good coffee and kept the cigarette supply well stocked—two very important staples of life.

Next Jude casually brought up the cab driver who recently harassed her, and told me how mad she was at him. She had nothing to report, when I asked her, about contacting the authorities about his actions. She seemed to express less anger than usual, but made it known in no uncertain terms that she "missed her Angel kids." Then she mentioned that she had an appointment to see the dentist to fix some abscesses and told me, with conviction, that she was "too young for false teeth."

Session Thirty-Four

Since our last visit, Jude had again been to a hospital in the city to see a neurologist to help assess damages from her accident. This visit made her very angry for it brought up memories of being in the hospital and subjected to the loss of her family and freedom.

It was a beautiful spring day and Jude was wearing sandals. I noticed that she had a smashed and bleeding toe. When I asked her how she had injured it and if it hurt, she brushed me off. It made me wonder if she had any feeling in her foot. The smashed toe brought me back to an awareness of her degrading living conditions, for I imagined her falling over the clutter outside her apartment. I felt inspired to offer an escape from her dark and crowded front room and go to a local park at the harbor. Jude thought this was a great idea, especially because I had brought my dog along.

At the park I helped Jude over a concrete barrier in the parking lot. The dog bounded around us and we looked, in my mind, for all the world like two unremarkable people going for a walk in the park with their dog. Unremarkable, except for the fact that the woman walked with a noticeably jerky gait.

Before we sat on the grass, I helped Jude light her fire against the wind and she comfortably settled in to tell me, yet again, in detail how she hated her ex-husband and younger brother for taking away her children and freedom. This anger, highlighted by the brisk ocean wind, was especially precise and lucid. I felt that I was in the presence of a person who knew her mind and had a clear and realistic idea of how she had sustained her losses. Always the grieving mother, Jude peppered her story with the lament of how she wanted her children back.

After hearing Jude's story of loss, I stood up and helped her to her feet. The dog came over with a stick in its mouth and teased me by growling and turning its head when I tried to grab the stick. I spontaneously demanded the stick by playfully commanding "Gimme that thang!" Jude lit up and echoed my command to the dog with bemusement. Whispering my words again, she informed me that "Gimme that thang!" was *exactly the phrase Crazy Bill used to command sticks from his and Jude's dogs during the heyday of their marital bliss!* I had no idea that I had uttered such evocative words, and was grateful for the serendipitous nature of our sessions to allow Jude to experience herself in such an immediate, complete, and joyous manner.

"Gimme that thang!" was a phrase that retained the power to evoke memories of better times—without the emotions of grief. We used it, out of the context of dogs and sticks, in future sessions to pull Jude out of emotional landslides. Consequently it became part of our private therapeutic language, along with her songs and mantras.

Jude was so relaxed by the end of our session that she told me she might not need counseling if she got her teeth fixed and a new house. Neither of these events had taken place so I could only wait to see if this were true.

Session Thirty-Five

When I arrived at Jude's I could see by her agitated state that something was wrong. Before she asked me about my "Angel family" she blurted out with wide eyes "Philip beat the fuck out of me!" This news stunned me and I asked her to show me the marks. She could not produce any evidence of bodily harm, only damage to the walls in the bedroom. It looked like she and Philip had a row of some sort without physical contact. I called Paul directly and found out that he knew of the supposed battle with Philip.

Paul suspected that the obscene graffiti on, and holes in Jude's bedroom walls were the products of her son Bobby, even though they might have expressed the sentiments of his mother.

"FUCK YOU PHILIP," "PHILIP ASSHOLE," and crude drawings of penises and vaginas were scrawled on the walls around several fist and foot sized holes smashed in the drywall. The room certainly bore the marks of rage. I thought of Paul's conjecture that the graffiti and damage might have been the work of Bobby because the letters of the words, though crudely written, showed no indication of a shaky Huntington's afflicted hand. The evidence of unleashed fury in the bedroom also did not fit with my recent experience of Jude's emotional state. Obviously someone who lacked emotional control was very angry with Philip. When I asked Jude if she had been responsible for the damage to the room, she immediately took credit for the writing and said that Philip had made the holes in the walls. I didn't believe her and invited her to write "FUCK YOU PHILIP" on my note pad. She did, and produced wavy lined letters that showed none of the control of those inscribed on her bedroom walls. Then, when I asked if Bobby had done the writing and/or holes, she flatly denied that he had been at her house in the past week.

Suddenly Jude expressed a great deal of anger toward those whom she perceived to have used her. She singled out Philip, who freely used and dirtied her pillows and towels, and stayed at her place without paying rent or contributing to her household in any way. She also took a few shots at Sandy whom she felt had been paid to ruin her teeth and neglect her needs.

I pondered this latest disturbance in Jude's life and came to the conclusion that it was not the manifestation of an isolated relationship with Philip, but connected to the core of her deepest angst—her separation from her children.

Bobby, her oldest son at 14, was not allowed by his father and stepmother to visit Jude when he wished. This unfortunate situation must have created a highly charged attraction between the artificially disconnected mother and child. Consequently Bobby visited his mother without his father's knowledge, and Jude idealized the sweetness of her stolen time with him. The reality of the situation was that Bobby abused his relationship with Jude by stealing money from her and exploiting her inclination to look the other way.

I figured that when Bobby got wind of Philip's abuse of the hospitality he felt was rightfully his, he became insanely jealous and stepped in to claim his territory and take out his rage on the walls of Philip's bedroom. Jude's passionate devotion to her children compelled her to take the fall for her son's vandalism of her apartment. After thinking about it I was glad that I had not gone to the police and reported Philip for abusing Jude and vandalizing the bedroom. Philip, like his predecessor, Karen, soon disappeared from Jude's life, and I never saw nor heard from him again. Bobby, however continued to be a troubling presence in his mother's life.

Session Thirty-Six

A life can move from darkness to light as quickly as clouds are blown from the face of the sun. Jude looked pert today, puffing away on a cigarette, after removal by an oral surgeon of all her teeth. She opened her mouth wide and proudly showed me her stitched up gums. She was delighted that *something had finally been done* to provide relief from the constant pain of her infections. This tangible evidence of positive support from her social safety net, though a long time coming, proved profoundly transforming.

She next informed me that she had decided to forgive her younger brother John, "even though he was a bad boy"—and then extended her forgiveness to her lawyer, Robin Gower. Needless to say this change of heart was landmark evidence of real progress in the melting of her resentment.

The removal of Jude's teeth was not the only positive news of the week. Paul had engineered a move from the despicable apartment to a cheerful little house just down the street. Jude was beside herself with excitement and begged me to take a walk over to see her new home. It was just as she described, a small bright house on a gracious lot with plenty of windows and garden space.

I wondered how rapidly Jude would heal, now that the major conditions of her much needed upgrading of health and living conditions had been met. Forgiving her brother and the lawyer proved only to be the beginning.

Jude was very proud that she had controlled her anger and not used swear words in a recent visit with her lawyer. I complimented her on her ability to behave appropriately around authority, and inferred that displaying such behavior might help convince those in control of her life that she was responsible enough to have more contact with her children. She laughed derisively and said she'd do better if she kidnapped her daughters. I told her what a very bad idea I thought that was, and offered the suggestion that she invite her estranged daughters over for tea in her new house to show them how non-threatening and together she was. Then she might win them back in a positive manner and impress the authorities with her responsibility. Jude said she loved this idea and told me in detail all about the tea she would serve.

I listened and supported her plans knowing that she was terrified of being rejected by her daughters, who had already chosen to have nothing to do with her because of the outspoken bitterness and destructive behavior she displayed after her brain injury. If this reconciliation were to occur, it would probably be some time after she had reestablished herself as a more solid and positive person.

Next, Jude asked me to beat up her ex-husband, Brent. I laughed and told her that beating people up was *not* in my job description. She seemed to easily accept my response and told me that Paul had said the same thing when asked.

Session Thirty-Seven

This was my first visit with Jude in her new house! Paul had skillfully organized the move without losing or seeming to mistreat any of the shrine or precious mementos. The process of unpacking looked to be proceeding slowly and methodically. The parts of the shrine that were already set up were displayed on shelves in an orderly fashion—a far cry from the overwhelming pile in the front room of her old apartment.

Jude's new house provided a larger, more attractive, and more functional living space than her old dwelling and seemed to immediately inspire her to take better care of her surroundings. A case in point was the placement of a throw rug in front of the couch to catch errant coals and protect the wall-to-wall carpeting from burns. I was impressed and gratified to see that she was capable of displaying the attributes of a "good housekeeper" *if she cared for her environment.*

Jude was so happy that she forgot to lament the loss of her children. This was indeed a first! I feared she might have lost herself in euphoria, like she had in darkness and rage, and was somewhat relieved by her ability to ground herself through singing her mantras. The mantra for the day, and for months to follow, was "Heaven, I'm in Heaven." I bobbed along and kept an eye out for trouble in paradise.

Session Thirty-Eight

My second visit to Jude in her new home found her tending the environment with the same care and respect I had seen on my last. Now that the immediate novelty of being in her new house had worn off a bit, she was able take some pride in how she was keeping the place. This pride was a very positive sign of progress in the restoration of her self-image because she needed to be able to experience herself in the role of an effective housekeeper to see herself as accomplished—and *real*.

Even though she was in her wonderful new house, Jude still felt her losses. She told me several times in the course of our session that she missed her "Angel kids."

However she had not forgotten that she had forgiven her younger brother John, and told me that she was depending on him to help her get a phone in her new house. I pointed out that the channel for his help was now opened wider by her forgiveness. This was proof of the lesson I had been trying to impress upon her since we started working together: *that love and forgiveness open doors while bitterness and hate close them.*

When I first met Jude this important distinction was lost to her because she was overwhelmed with the emotions of her grief. In this earlier state she could *only* see herself as a victim. It seemed she was presently able to participate in life as a person who was capable of forgiving those who previously had victimized her.

Now that we had achieved the satisfaction of having received medication for her Huntington's disease, treatment of her abscesses, and improved living conditions, I asked Jude what else she wished to have done on her behalf. She told me, predictably, that she wanted her Angel kids back. She also mentioned that she wanted to start a therapeutic camp for disabled and disadvantaged children.

When I asked her what her camp would look like she replied without hesitation, "Animal rides, farm and fun!" I pushed her a bit by asking if she thought "they" would let her do it and she answered with complete certainty, "Yes! Because *we* need it!"

The idea of starting a therapeutic farm for children was an old dream of Jude's that I had heard about from Paul, and that she counted on being able to manifest with the money won in her lawsuit against the man who ran her over. Now that she had forgiven her lawyer, she felt closer to making her dream come true.

Our conversation about realizing dreams somehow inspired Jude to tease me by asking if I wanted to watch strippers at a local bar. This seeming non sequitur prompted me to try to engage her in a serious talk about how my feelings on the objectification of women kept me from enjoying strip bars as much as she thought I might. This was all too much for Jude, and she shut me up by informing me that I probably didn't need to go to a strip bar because I had a wife!

Even though Jude had forgiven two important people on her hate list, she still retained anger at others, and wanted me to know how angry she remained at Philip, Brent and Mara. She took her time and gave me a blow-by-blow history of her problems with these three people.

It was clear from this history that Jude was feeling vulnerable and still deeply grieving the loss of her family. After listening, I knew that we still had some way to go before her heart was healed.

Session Thirty-Nine

Jude greeted me with her usual "Hi Santa! How's your Angel family?" and could hardly wait for my answer before she excitedly launched into telling me, "Bobby's in jail for stealing a chocolate bar!" It sounded plausible to me that he may have been caught shoplifting—but thrown in jail for it?

When I pressed her for more details concerning Bobby's incarceration, Jude changed the subject, listing Bobby's problems with Brent and Mara. This list was peppered with swearing, summed up in the outspoken sentiment, "Fuck them! Shit!"

I suppose she felt responsible for Bobby's problems and got relief from her guilt by reviling his caretakers for not doing the parenting she felt *she* was capable of—but couldn't because of the fact that she had lost the right to care for her own children. She was, however, looking forward to a meeting with Paul and the probation department, next month, to see if she could help resolve Bobby's problems with the law.

It was a beautiful sunny afternoon and Jude's house sparkled with order and cleanliness. While she proudly showed me the new towels and cleaning tools Paul had brought her earlier in the week, she sang, "Heaven, I'm in Heaven!"

We decided to go out into the yard to enjoy the day. Jude threw sticks for my dog and hollered, "Gimme that thang!" when the dog teased her with the stick.

After a while of playing with the animal, Jude grew wistful and started crying over losing Crazy Bill. Her straightforward grieving of this loss was a true and healthy expression of her sorrow and bore absolutely no bitterness or attitude of self-pity. She was even inspired to express thankfulness for "all the good" in her life. This was a remarkable turn-around for someone who was so despondent less than a year ago that she had tried to take her own life.

Jude's personal grooming also displayed her positive turn of mood, for she was usually now freshly showered and in clean clothes when I visited her. She also had recently taken to having her hair done and ranged from looking chic and appropriate to strange and somewhat macabre, depending on the skill of the person who helped her style it. She looked best when she did it herself, and I had to wonder about the tastes and motives of some of her other stylists.

Things were definitely looking up and she told me a number of times during our session, "My heart *is* getting better!" Another indication of the remarkable change in Jude's condition was the fact that she had recently called her brother John, and the lawyer, to thank them for her "beautiful new life."

At one point I might have thought that Jude's present level of good nature and ability to forgive those she so recently hated were as far as we could hope to go, but I felt that there was more to come. Jude's newfound forgiveness included her brother and lawyer. These two people were deemed enemies only by their association with events that resulted in the loss of her family and autonomy. They were the easy ones because they had committed no concrete acts against her. We still had to forgive the doctor, judge, Sandy, and most importantly, Brent and Mara, who were actively involved in the removal of her children from her life.

It seemed we had reached a plateau about half way to completely freeing Jude from her bitterness. Happily, the most therapeutic way to reach our goal of a healed heart was to celebrate and enjoy the fruits of our labors.

Session Forty

Jude caught me completely off guard by flashing me a smile of her newly acquired false teeth. These "chompers," as I came to call them, never did seem to fit quite right in her mouth because of the constant motion of her lower jaw. The process of fitting the new teeth to Jude's mouth was somewhat drawn out, as she was destined to see the dentist repeatedly and never could wear the full set in her mouth. Even so she persevered with the uppers and I grew used to her with a radiant smile that eventually complimented her sparkling eyes.

In spite of the fact that her son Bobby was not in her care, Jude was feeling enough like a responsible mother to have something to say about his behavior. It had come to her, through Paul, that Bobby was smoking pot and stealing money from stores and family members to buy it. This was indeed very disturbing information for a mother to hear about her child. Though Jude's expressed stance on the recreational smoking of marijuana was comparatively liberal, she was not at all comfortable with her children stealing to obtain it.

She told me that Bobby was not welcome in her house as long as he was "on pot" because she was afraid he would steal from her as well. Her best advice to her son, at this time, was to "just say no to drugs!"

It impressed me that Jude, who was so desperate for her children's company, would consider putting up a boundary that prohibited visits from her beloved son. Though this was a good sign of her returning ability to act as a responsible parent, I was not sure how firmly she would be able to stand against Bobby if he pushed her to accept him—pot and all.

Jude was delighted that her youngest son, Jamie, had helped Paul unload some heavy boxes of her diet supplement into her kitchen. Jamie saw Jude more, on supervised visits with Paul, than any of her other children. His helping Paul unload the heavy boxes was heart rending because it reminded her that she was missing his growing up and prompted her, once again, to tell me how much she missed her Angel kids. As usual, I simply acknowledged her loss by saying, "I know, sweetheart, I know."

After this dip into grief, Jude told me, with great excitement, how a neighbor was going to help her plant strawberries and blueberries in her backyard. She went on to elaborate, in detail, how she would use her harvest of berries to make pancakes. We sat around chanting, "yum…pancakes, yum…pancakes…" until it was clear that we might drive ourselves crazy with anticipation.

Jude had been busy keeping her environment tidy, and wanted to impress upon me how much she loved her new home by showing me how clean it was—"clean, clean, clean." I was duly impressed with the consistency of good housekeeping that I observed on my regular visits. I was also gratified to have the opportunity to see the answer to my earlier question of how Jude would care for a dwelling that she actually liked. My hunch that the poor treatment of her previous apartment had much to do with her hatred of the place because she was moved there against her will, seemed not far off the mark.

The home care workers, whom I occasionally met coming and going, complained that Jude was still a "poor housekeeper" and that what I saw on my visits was the fruit of their labors. I suspected that their opinions, as mine, were colored by their personal standards of household tidiness. Nevertheless the change in the state of Jude's environment, between her old apartment and new house, was as remarkable as the change in her mood from the time I first met her to the present.

More evidence of the positive change in Jude was her increasing ability to let me go after the end of our one-hour sessions. When I first met her, she would physically hold onto me, as I went out the door, yelling, "You can't go!…You can't go!" After a couple of times of literally prying myself from her grip, I picked up the phrase and started chanting, "Oh no! You can't go!…Oh no! You can't go!…Oh no! You can't go!…" just as I was about to leave her home. After some painful good-byes, Jude eventually began to chant along with me. It seemed that the chant absorbed some of the pain of her perceived abandonment. Over time her attachment to my being with her had grown less and less urgent until now, when the ease of my departure was so unprecedented that I underscored it in my session notes.

Session Forty-One

It took only one short week of barring Bobby from her home for Jude to lose her anger at him and inform me that she was "not pissed at Bobby anymore." I did not expect her to keep up Bobby's banishment, because of her expressed need to have her children with her. She was ready to take Bobby back, warts and all.

Letting Bobby back into her home *was* the obvious thing to do from her perspective, but came with its share of challenges as one would expect from harboring a distraught teenager who was bent on exploiting his vulnerable mother. In my opinion, the whole situation reeked of danger and threatened Jude's newly emerging equilibrium.

Jude was busy shoring up her newfound happiness, singing, "Heaven, I'm in Heaven!" over and over during my visit. This particular mantra seemed to function at a different level than most of the others I had become familiar with over the past months. First of all, it was an affirmation of her state of being that was based on her perception of reality—not on a projection of her faith.

"Heaven, I'm in Heaven!" was the only one of Jude's mantras that I did *not* sing along with. The change in her life from Hell to Heaven was hers, not mine. I felt that I could join in her prayers and be part of her cheering section, but did not want to usurp her perception, either positive or negative. So, when she sang the "Heaven" mantra, I simply bobbed my head and told her how happy *I* was for her. When I asked in what ways her life had become Heaven, she referred to her new teeth, house, home-life, and medication.

Jude told me how she had met a girlfriend at the Angel House whom she used to trade babysitting with in the old days before her accident. Her exchange with this friend sounded much like the normal exchange of two friends meeting each other after a long time apart. I was pleased to see that Jude's bitterness had receded to a point where it did not stand in the way of her comfortably reconnecting with someone from her past. At least she made it sound pleasant. I wasn't there so I didn't hear if, or how vigorously, she dumped her woes on her old buddy.

She also reported meeting a man in a wheelchair, with whom she was striking up a new friendship. She showed me a stuffed penguin and said that this new friend had given it to her. She called both the man and the penguin "Honey". I hoped that this man, whom she met on a walk, might become a genuine friend, and was not out to exploit her good nature.

It always struck me how vulnerable Jude was in the world, and I found myself grieving the lack of basic safety she and other visibly disabled people find in public. Mind you, I am the kind of person who gets upset every time I have to use a key to lock something up from a population that has thrown the Ten Commandments out the window!

Nevertheless, Jude looked sleek and healthy in the relative safety of her new home. Her complexion was rosy and she was showing her new smile around like it was bursting from her mouth. It was, in fact, busily separating from her gums because of the constant movement of her jaw. She eventually took out her new teeth and carefully put them in a glass to soak, promising me that she was going to attach them later with "Super Glue."

She told me that, while she was walking home from the Angel House, she spontaneously decided to forgive her ex-husband Brent. She said, in all seriousness, "I just got to forgive the Asshole for being such a Dick!" Of course I received this as great news and made a big fuss over it by telling her how I thought this kind of forgiveness really healed the heart. Jude then said that she believed in a "Loving God." Now I waited to see what kind of real action this act of forgiveness would inspire in her interaction with Brent and his family.

Session Forty-Two

Jude was beside herself with joy because Bobby had come over to visit her on Mother's Day. She was singing her "Heaven, I'm in Heaven" mantra. This mantra seemed to have replaced "Jesus loves me, this I know" in the number one spot on her hit parade. I wondered how long this light mood would last and wasn't left to wonder long when she clearly told me, with some ceremony, "My heart is getting healed." If this were really the case, she was well on the way to having no more need of my services.

Jude was able to talk about Brent without being overwhelmed by anger and bitterness. She told me that she "married him to have kids."

While she was talking I noticed, for the first time, that her left arm and hand were molded into a fixed position that stood out in great contrast to the exaggerated animation of the rest of her body. It also looked to me like a characteristic post-paralytic symptom of brain injury, which I have observed in many clients and myself. Her right arm jerked around as usual, but eventually came to rest peacefully on her lap after several minutes of concentrated talking.

Again I felt closer to distinguishing the elusive boundary between her brain injury and Huntington's disease. I was aware that it may have been there for me to see all along, and wondered if it were now easier to see because of the calming nature of Dr. Keller's drugs.

But it was not only the physical manifestations of her two interwoven disabilities that were becoming visible to me. These manifestations were reflections of the confusing nature of their figure-ground relationship. *Maybe Jude was becoming so whole, through her process of therapy and recovery, that I could better distinguish the relativity of her dual disabilities against the background of her more emotionally stable personality.*

In keeping with her light mood, she reminisced about coming nose to nose with a black bear on a childhood camping trip with her foster sister. The story, especially the details of her sister's reaction, was hilarious and we had a good laugh over it.

Before I left, Bobby dropped in to see his mother. He looked healthy, self-assured, and appeared to have remembered me from a visit of many months ago at Jude's last apartment. He almost seemed too good to be true and was doing a good job of hiding his troubles—not to mention his fear of knowing that he had a 50/50 chance of carrying the Huntington's gene. I would have loved to have worked with him, but the company that hired me to counsel Jude had turned down Paul's requests to use my services as a family counselor.

Session Forty-Three

The first thing out of Jude's mouth was, "I miss my Angel kids!" Again, I only quietly replied "I know sweetheart, I know." I imagined she would be expressing this sentiment over and over until she got her children back. I had my doubts whether she would ever be deemed responsible enough to have them returned to her care, but nonetheless reassured her that I thought she was well on the way to reestablishing fulfilling relationships with her family. I made it clear to Jude that I might be talking a matter of years and she seemed able to accept my projection, in that moment, without impatience.

Even though she had decided to forgive Brent and Mara, Jude was still busy processing her negative feelings about them. She told me that she used to hire Mara to baby-sit her children, and mused in amazement, "She (Mara) was just 12 years old!" Then she went on and thundered indignantly "They (Brent and Mara) made love in *my* shower!" Jude capped off these memories of her ex-husband's infidelity with the babysitter with a lusty "I hate them!"

I listened to this story with appropriate shock and sympathy and then dared to ask her, "How can you forgive them, if you hate them?" She had a ready answer for this question and told me that she had to make peace with the caregivers of her children if she ever expected to participate more in their upbringing. I translated this to mean that Jude would do almost anything to get her kids back into her life—maybe even love her enemies.

There was only one other craving, besides the need to have her children back, that Jude seemed powerless against—her need for cigarettes. At the moment she found herself out of smokes and asked me if I would walk her down to the corner store and buy her some.

I usually don't lavish money or gifts on my clients because I want them to have no confusion over why I am there. My gift is the ability to help them recover themselves, and I do not believe that I have to bribe them to accept my presence in their lives. Sometimes I bring homemade crafts or artwork, like my wife's Angel picture, but only if I feel it enhances the therapeutic process.

Today's request for cigarettes inspired me to relax my boundaries and we took a walk to the corner convenience store. Jude seemed well known to the store personnel and immediately went outside in the parking lot to light up after our purchase. I was a bit uncomfortable buying the cigarettes because of the niggling feeling that I was acting like an indulgent parent. She was appropriately thankful and announced, when we arrived back at her house, "I'm like a daughter to you!"

Session Forty-Four

Jude was thrilled that she had been able to organize, with help from her friend at the Angel House, the purchase of a fifty-dollar ghetto blaster for her son Jamie. This was an immense expenditure for her and she greatly enjoyed telling me how she had gathered and spent the money on this gift. I felt she was talking to me like one relatively affluent parent to another.

The house was *still* sparkling clean and, I believe, a reliable reflection of Jude's inner state. I was starting to feel a definite swing towards a more lasting state of positive healing, hearing her express, almost exclusively, that her heart was "being fixed"—and not "broken." In fact, she happily volunteered for the first time that it was indeed healed, by exclaiming, "Thank you Santa for fixing my heart!" I did not take this to mean that our work was done, but only as an immediate expression of her relief in the progress of our therapy.

By this time Jude was feeling so relaxed that she traded her usual mantras for singing "Willie and the Hand Jive." We hooted with laughter and slapped our legs in rhythm with the song. Then she asked me to bring a guitar on my next visit so that we could really get into it. The prospect of playing music with me brought back the memory of an old boyfriend who was in a band that Jude ran soundboard for.

Though she was feeling positive and secure, it was not enough to override her anxiety about not being a good mother to her children. Jude was very concerned that Jamie was being picked on in school. She became aware of her son's school time difficulties from Paul when he brought him over. Knowing that I raised four boys, she asked me if my kids had had the same problem when they were in school. I traded stories with her and was glad to see that she related to me as just another parent, sharing stories and ideas. This was more evidence of progress in the restoration of her self-image as a functional parent.

Session Forty-Five

Since Jude seemed to have got everything she had been asking for, I asked her what, if anything, she would change about her life. She immediately answered, "Nothing, it's perfect except my Angel kids aren't here!" This was pretty much what I expected and showed me that she was about as satisfied as she could be, under the circumstances.

Then she went on to remark about her youngest son, "Jamie spoils me rotten!"-referring to the attention he lavished upon her during his visits with Paul. This prompted a chorus of "Heaven, I'm in Heaven" followed by a few "Praise the Lords!" and a heartfelt rendition of "Kumbai ya." I joined in on "Kumbai ya" and we sang away for about ten minutes.

Next Jude was inspired to tell me about an old friend and Harley rider who used to bug her to go out with him until she had to firmly say, "No, I'm with Bill!" She wanted me to know that she was a "one man woman, and didn't sleep around!"

Curiously she didn't leave it there and went on to describe her old friend's horses, adding that she wanted to someday be with horses again. This was a partially realized wish for Sandy had, at one time, taken her riding at a local therapeutic riding society. Then she said, "I would love to work with horses when I grow up!"

I asked her if she weren't already grown up and, if in fact she were, what her work was. She answered without hesitation, "A mother!" Then told me again about having babies and how it was all she ever really wanted to do in life.

Jude lamented that her first husband, Rick, didn't want to have children because he thought that he had been a "bad boy" when he was younger. Apparently he was afraid that he would have troublesome kids because of the bad karma he created through his wayward actions as a youth.

I told her that I was sorry because I knew how much she loved Rick, and that my understanding of karma was not fully developed enough to know whether his reasoning was sound. She laughed and said she had got her kids anyway!

Session Forty-Six

Jude was not at home when I arrived at her house. This was very unusual and I waited outside on her porch. She showed up about ten minutes later, walking down the sidewalk sporting a fancy new haircut that looked professionally done. I guess since the sun was shining, and she felt that she looked like a million bucks, she had decided to show herself off to the neighborhood. Though I lathered her with compliments and plied her with questions, she grew coy and would not tell me who had given her the haircut.

Later I noticed and remarked that Jude's false teeth were green with some kind of leftover food. She promptly took them out and went to the bathroom to clean them. She certainly seemed to be paying more attention than usual to her looks. This was wonderful to see for it reflected that she was feeling good enough to see herself, and want to be seen by others, as a vital and attractive woman. Jude's clothes were mostly utilitarian, but she did wear colorful scarves and always had bangles on her arms that jangled along with her movements.

In spite of her good feelings about herself, she still told me that she missed her kids and emphasized that Bobby, who had been visiting often, "should be with his mommy." She spoke fondly of her son, saying, "He's a good guy!" and that she was very proud of him.

She also told me that she couldn't sleep at night because she stayed up missing her children. I knew of her sleeping problem, but this was the first time she had chosen to tell me what kept her up at night. It made me realize how important it was to keep grieving the loss of her children at the forefront of our work together. Then she said, "My heart is still broken—but getting better! Thank you Santa."

Next Jude went on a small rant against the insurance company I worked for. When I asked her why she was mad at them she said, "Because they charge so much for car insurance!" This was a very interesting answer because Jude didn't even drive a car anymore! All of my clients who receive rehabilitation benefits through the insurance company I work for have been injured in motor vehicle accidents. They usually complain about matters like delayed funding and not being adequately supported in their recovery—never about their insurance rates.

Maybe Jude was feeling so much like her old self that she temporarily forgot her disabilities. Amazing.

Once again I noticed that the house looked well respected and beautifully maintained. Jude also indicated that she was taking care of herself, by informing me how much she was looking forward to a massage appointment Paul was scheduled to take her to later in the afternoon.

She said she used the massage to relieve her aching back, a symptom she attributed to being struck by the car. When I asked her why she hadn't been going to massage all along, she heartily answered, "That's what I wonder, too!"

I experienced the moment of our minds meeting in indignation over the fact that she had not previously received massage therapy as a breakthrough in our therapy. Here, she was able to come together with me in mutual indignation around the highly sensitive issue of her mistreatment by the system, without the triggering of uncontrollable anger or bitterness.

Session Forty-Seven

This afternoon I was surprised and almost knocked over by a large golden retriever when I opened Jude's front door. She immediately informed me that the animal was her new dog, "Crillo—maybe I should have named him Harley." When I asked where she got the dog Jude replied, "From an Angel bro!" Evidently someone had simply given her the dog.

I was not sure whether having a big furry animal was such a good idea because it might throw off the delicate balance of Jude's questionable housekeeping abilities. I looked around and saw that the place, though not as clean as usual, was in relatively good order, even though it was now littered by matted fur and scattered piles of wood splinters that "Crillo" had deposited from chewing sticks in the house.

Jude seemed comfortable with the additional mess and I hoped that she would get to it later. I feared the constant work of cleaning up after a pet might threaten to degrade her living conditions by being beyond her capability or overloading her home care workers. She also told me that the "dog hogs the bed" when she referred to its sleeping with her. If nothing else, I was glad she had found a live-in companion who wasn't consciously bent on exploiting her kindness. I was also heartened to see that Jude was feeling well enough to want to take on the responsibility of a canine companion.

Paul told me he was highly doubtful of Jude's capacity to be responsible for an animal. He worried specifically about her ignoring shopping for herself and spending all her meager budget on food and treats for the dog. His assessment of her inclination to overindulge a pet, at the expense of her own needs, struck me as presumptuous—though not mean spirited.

Because I had no first hand knowledge of Jude's ability to run a household without support from Paul and her legion of home care workers, I did not dismiss his opinion lightly. Actually, I was invested in preparing Jude to present herself to the world as a responsible person and did not want to automatically credit opinions or evidence that contradicted the momentum of our work. My attitude might have been imprudent if children were present, but only really threatened the well being of a stray dog and several cats who sometimes relied on her hospitality.

Some weeks ago Jude had given me permission to consult with a previous lawyer who had represented her in a pre-accident legal battle with Brent for her children. During this consultation I had the opportunity to read documents drawn from interviews that described her as an overindulgent parent who was not quite grounded in the responsibility of raising children. Regardless of the truth in these reports, no one disputed the fact that she lavished love on her family and maintained a functional household—even if it did not meet everyone's expectations of discipline and cleanliness. All in all, I was pleased that Jude felt she had enough love and energy to care for another being besides herself, and took it as a sign of her returning ability to be a nurturing and responsible caregiver.

Introducing me to her new dog rekindled Jude's memories of her pre-accident family life and she told me that she still missed her Angel kids. Then she went on to talk about how she had mourned the loss of Crazy Bill at his funeral ten years ago, and that she yearned for an "old man and a family again."

She informed me that she had seen "bad girl Sandy" at a local brain injury conference, but it seemed that she used the words "bad girl" merely as descriptive terms and I sensed no negative emotional charge. Was she getting ready to finally forgive Sandy along with her brother, the lawyer, and Brent?

Session Forty-Eight

When I arrived at Jude's house "Crillo" was not to be seen. I asked her where the dog was and she told me it had "run away." She said she missed "Crillo" but did not seem distraught. The house looked well lived in but cleaner than last week, without the dog's leavings. Jude was trying to wear her lower teeth but had to remove them because they impeded her speech. Once she got the lower dentures out of her mouth, she proceeded to give me a review of her three husbands and an old suitor.

Rick Banks, her first husband, was described as an "overall good guy." Brent, the second and father of three of her children, was a "bad guy who took my kids away." Crazy Bill, the third, was her great love and his loss sorely grieved. The old suitor she mentioned was named Peter, and Jude expressed some regret that she didn't marry him after separating from Rick.

Jude's reminiscences also included stories of her brother Wade and his wife Darin. Darin was close to Jude and they used to "burn up the telephone lines between Alberta and B.C."

Jude said she missed her "friendship" with her sister-in-law. She then reported that Darin left her brother and "broke his heart." "Now," Jude mused, "Darin is in a wheelchair!"

Jude wistfully told me these stories without swearing or expressing the need to discharge any grief through anger or sadness.

Session Forty-Nine

Jude started out in a good mood and immediately became very chatty, reminiscing about the time when I took her to the park with my dog. She repeated "Gimme that thang!" a few times and told me with relish, "We had a good time there!" She also asked me if my runaway cat had come home and showed great concern over its welfare. Jude knew about my missing cat from a previous session, when she led me in a long chant that went, "My meow meow won't come home...my meow meow won't come home..."

The fact that Jude chose to reminisce about magical moments of *our* relationship, even if they did remind her of her life with Crazy Bill, showed me she was becoming comfortable enough with her life *in the present* to want to celebrate its good moments through chants, mantras, and anecdotes. She also told me over and over that Jamie spoiled her rotten when he came with Paul to visit.

In the midst of this seeming contentment, Jude brought up how much she missed her kids and Crazy Bill. Though she still felt the need to express her grief, I felt it was becoming a more tolerable part of her every waking moment.

I took the opportunity, after her expression of loss, to ask Jude about the state of her heart. She cautiously replied that her heart was "getting better, but not completely healed." I asked her if this was "bullshit" and she emphatically told me, "No bullshit! It *is* getting better!" She went on to sing her "Praise Jesus" mantra, stopped, then started to quietly chortle "fuck fuck fuck." like a tired little chicken.

While I was at the house, a young man came by to service her new cable TV hook-up. Jude immediately engaged him in a conversation about Harley-Davidson motorcycles. I mused that the serviceman might have thought we were a couple, and was impressed that Jude straightened him out about the professional nature of our relationship when I heard her voluntarily refer to me as her counselor.

After the serviceman left, Jude told me she wanted to reduce her smoking from about three packs a day to only three or four cigarettes. I didn't know what precipitated this desire to cut down, but encouraged her even though I doubted she would be successful. It was a remarkable sign of her increasing ability to control her life.

Session Fifty

At the moment Jude's mantras were in full flower. She was singing more than talking and it seemed to me that the protective screen of her magical verses was diffusing any factual communication between us. Suddenly, she broke free of her chanting and told me, "I miss my kids!" I returned with my usual "I know, sweetheart, I know." Then she looked at me, smiled, and began to sing in a wee little voice, "You are my sunshine…"

She next told me about walking over to a local cafe every morning for coffee, saying about the people she saw there daily, "They are my family, my home!" I asked her how she felt about the Angel House, which she also visited often. She replied, "They are my home too!" Then, gesturing to his picture over the couch, Jude told me how much she missed Crazy Bill and said, "They don't make 'em like that anymore."

As her court case was coming up in the new year, we talked a bit about the possibility of an award and Jude told me, with some excitement, that she was going to get "950 million dollars!" This was, of course, an outrageously high estimate and I asked her why so much? She easily answered, "Because they owe it to me!"

Jude perceived herself to have been grievously injured and, in her mind, no price was too high to equal the amount of her suffering. I let it go, and did not push my opinion of how unrealistic her expectations of British Columbia's legal system might be. I tried to help her understand that, although she had a lawyer championing her cause, when the time came she would get what she would get and there wasn't much either of us could do about it.

After the talk about her lawsuit, Jude told me once more that she missed her Angel kids and that her heart still hurt even though it was getting better. She still expressed some anger at the insurance company, but I experienced it as only an expression of remaining low-level generic anger.

Exploring her legal situation did not set Jude off into a black mood as it might have done earlier in our counseling relationship. She was, to the contrary, in a fine mood and showed me the copper bracelet that she wore on her arm. I complimented her on how beautiful I thought it looked on her, and she smiled coyly and told me that she wore it to keep from getting arthritis. I asked her how she knew that and she answered, "I just heard about it from someone." This kind of casual small talk once again demonstrated her ability to carry on like a person who was not so overwhelmed by tragedy and disease that she had to talk about it, or related matters, all the time.

Jude also mentioned that her teeth moving around had created a sore in her mouth. She spontaneously got up and went into the washroom to glue them in during our session. When she came back she actually sang, "Come on baby light my fire!" while I lit her first cigarette of the session.

In spite of our good-natured chatting Jude still held on to her anger. "This is bullshit! Having my accident!" she finally yelled near the end of our session. Then she sang, "My meow meow won't come back," slapping her thighs in rhythm with the chant and diffusing the anger in a matter of seconds.

Session Fifty-One

Jude seemed a bit disconnected, and I wondered if I weren't perceiving her that way because of something Paul had put in my mind. Paul had recently consulted with me about what he suspected were increasing indications of dementia caused by Jude's advancing Huntington's disease. Though it was not my focus of attention, I couldn't put it out of the realm of possibility because of my ignorance or wishful thinking.

The cause of today's symptoms was soon revealed when she informed me that she had been out of smokes since last night and was "having a nic fit, honey!"

I drove her to a nearby convenience store and, for the second time in our relationship, bought her a pack of cigarettes. I also threw in a cheap plastic lighter as a bonus. I could see Jude standing by the car through the window of the store while I bought her smokes. Her movements were unusually pronounced. After I came out we lit her first cigarette in the parking lot and it immediately smoothed out her behavior, movements and all.

When we arrived at the house, Jude revealed that Bobby had been over and was putting the heat on her to give him money. Paul, who had a much better knowledge of this situation than I, was recommending to Jude that she call the police in to protect herself from her son.

Jude was offended by the idea that she might need protection from her own son, and insisted that Bobby needed "more love, not police, to act better." She said she was not afraid of Bobby yelling at her and making demands. I asked her what she was going to do as the mother of a troubled teenager. She responded that she would "just say no" to his demands. I thought this was wishful thinking complicated by the guilt and anger inherent in her and Bobby's unfortunate separation. Due to the limitations of my mandate to work with her and her family, I could only fall back and let the relationship play itself out. It did not promise to be a happy situation.

On the way out I bumped into a home care worker on her way in. She informed me with the now well-known complaint that Jude was a "bad house-keeper." She also said she could now talk with Jude about situations that previously triggered rage, like the state of her brother Wade in the hospital. She was a witness of Jude's progress in reducing the crippling anger and rage that had previously sabotaged her relationships.

Session Fifty-Two

Jude told me four or five times during our session that she missed her kids. She also mentioned that she missed Crazy Bill. I listened to her saying the same thing over and over and finally had the insight that *she may be spending time missing her loved ones so that she can have them in her mind while she is missing them.* Jude was happy to report that she had seen Jamie playing with Paul's daughter who came along with him on a recent visit. This made her feel like a real mother who had the pleasure of watching her child socialize with another of his own age group.

The usual spiritually toned mantras gave way to a chorus of "Born to be Wild." She went on to rant about how that "Asshole Brent" had made her sell her beloved Fender guitar for money. She also complained that he made her sell her old wedding and engagement rings. In this context the word "Asshole" was merely illustrative and not indicative of an all-consuming and self-defining anger.

Session Fifty-Three

On this day Jude was so fast that I teased her about being "on speed." Her mind was sharp and her body movements were relatively fluid. I suppose she was far enough along in her recovery to be experiencing some good days along with the bad ones; otherwise I could find no reason for her especially good state of being.

Along with her bright mood came a show and tell of some birthday cards she had prepared, in her own hand, for Bobby and her daughters who had birthdays coming up soon. Jude seemed to have approached this project with competence and skills that reflected her returning abilities.

She excitedly showed me three enlarged copies of the tear stained and crumpled photograph of Crazy Bill, which Paul had repaired and photocopied onto larger card stock. These pictures were hung in three special locations in the house, where she went to mourn and remember her loved one.

She vented some more anger at Brent and told me how he "abused" her children, when they were together, by grounding them for no apparent reason. This complaint was voiced with appropriate emotion and reinforced her belief that she was a good mother, who disagreed with her onerous ex-mate about raising the kids.

Our talk of raising kids prompted Jude to reminisce, with my encouragement, about the extent of her freedom in the old days. She was nostalgic about her "Big Pontiac four door" and "Rusty Ford van"—but mostly proud of her independence. I asked her if she drove both the vehicles and she quipped, "No, silly! Not at the same time!"

Session Fifty-Four

Jude's teeth had a gooey white film over them. I thought it might be cleaning solution or denture glue that she had forgotten to clean off. I could not get a straight answer out of her concerning the condition of her teeth, and did not really care.

I was, however, intrigued by the funny faces she was making at me throughout our session. Her faces seemed connected to a private reminiscence and not the usual grimaces of her Huntington's disease. Jude was full of stories about her drinking and partying days. She told me, "I used to stay up all night but I don't drink or party now!" These stories of freedom and dissolution were peppered with the lament, "I sure miss my Angel kids!" She went on to report that Bobby was "being good," having stopped smoking, drugs, and drinking. I wondered how she knew, and feared that the resourceful teenager was pulling the wool over his mother's eyes.

By the end of our session Jude's Huntington's movements had slowed down and almost come to a complete stop. She informed me, just before I left, that she had given one of her cats the new name of "Angel Sammy."

Session Fifty-Five

Jude started out our session telling me that Bobby had visited her in the morning. Then she started chanting, "Miss him, love him, proud of him…miss him, love him, proud of him…" and informed me that she sang her "Heaven, I'm in Heaven" mantra with him. She sang the Heaven mantra about seeing Bobby and repeated "I sure miss my Angel kids" throughout our session. When I restated that losing her children was her greatest loss, Jude said she had wanted children since she was nine years old in spite of the fact that she knew she might carry the Huntington's gene.

It had recently been suggested by her occupational therapist that Jude learn to use a device called a "talking board," which would allow her to communicate when her Huntington's disease advanced to the point where she could no longer speak. She flat out rejected this offer and asked me to help her pray her disease away.

She began by saying, "Take it away Lord Jesus!" Then, "Lord Jesus can do it!" and repeated these prayers over and over. I nodded my head and rocked my body in time to her chanting.

Then she started to quietly sing *"Hey Jude, don't make it bad. Take a sad song and make it better. Remember, to let her into your heart, then you can start to make it better."* As I listened, it struck me that the line "Remember, to let *her* into your heart" seemed like it needed some change. I suggested that we substitute "them" for "her" so that she could visualize her children in her heart and use her love for *them* to generate positive change in her life. Also, I said, if her children were in her heart, they would always be with her and she wouldn't have to miss them so much. Jude was not impressed by my suggestion and told me so. The song, as written, offered her the opportunity to put her new image of herself into her heart and *heal herself!* This was much more powerful and went a long way toward consummating the transformation we had been working so hard to effect.

Session Fifty-Six

Jude was furious with Paul for calling the police to have Bobby barred from visiting her. He did this in response to the fact that Bobby broke into his mother's house over the past week and bullied her around, making demands for money. Though Jude admitted to Bobby's behavior, Paul could not convince her to draw the line with her son and went to the police, who placed a restraining order against him. Paul genuinely believed he had acted in Jude's best interests. Jude summed it up saying, "Paul broke my heart by taking Bobby away and it makes me feel better to be mad at him!" Now Paul, like Sandy before him, was a conduit and target for all her grief and anger.

She also irrationally blamed Paul for finding her a house that was too small for her family. In her mind he became an "Asshole" and the sole reason for all the unhappiness in her life. This was the first time I had witnessed the addition of someone Jude loved to the top of her hate list. Her anger was all encompassing and made me glad I had managed to escape her wrath.

Session Fifty-Seven

When I showed up, Bobby and a friend were just leaving the house to go fishing. Bobby's friend, Red, acted developmentally disabled and looked much older. Bobby was very friendly and looked great. I knew he was there in spite of his restraining order and wondered what he was up to. Paul dropped by after Bobby had left and wanted to apologize to Jude for hurting her. Jude called him an "Asshole" and did not accept his apology. Her anger was not convincing and I sensed that, though it was deeply connected to the loss of her children, it was a sham when directed at Paul. She used the word "Asshole" like one of her mantras.

Before he left, Jude thanked Paul for some cigarettes he brought her and unconsciously called him "Angel Paul."

Session Fifty-Eight

Jude looked great and the house was clean and in good order. Not surprisingly Bobby had convinced his mother to let Red stay in her house. Shortly after Red's arrival she was asking her son to kick him out because he "couldn't pay rent." Jude wouldn't tell me what other trouble she had with Red, but I assumed that he probably abused her hospitality in any number of other ways. She went on a bit calling Red an "Asshole" and I imagined his name being inscribed, along with Karen and Philip's, in the minor league of her hate list.

Jude was very proud that Bobby had promised her he would get rid of his troublesome friend, and called her boy a "special loving son." When I asked her how he got that way she replied, "Because I raised him right!" I was glad to see her taking credit for raising her children, even though she hadn't had a hand in it for several years.

Jude asked me, out of the blue, if I "ever had a nic fit honey?" I asked her if she had ever seen me smoke and she replied, "Never!" with a raspy authority that woke me once again to how solid and sure of herself she had become. I started to tell her about my career as a smoker and she stopped me, saying that I had told her before. She even remembered the brand I smoked and enjoyed telling me how much, for how long, and how long ago I quit smoking.

Jude sang often, including her favorite "Heaven, I'm in Heaven". We also sang "Kumbai ya" and "I don't want a pickle—just want to ride on my motor-sickle" by Arlo Guthrie. The Guthrie name brought our conversation to Huntington's disease and a question, which I couldn't answer, as to whether or not Arlo had inherited his father's disease.

Jude said her mother and grandmother, both of whom had Huntington's, encouraged her to have children. Then she remembered a highchair her grandmother had given her for a wedding present. Since Jude had no children with Rick, she used the highchair to support a houseplant. She beamed while she told me this story and I asked her if she ever felt alone.

She answered "I have a family but *not* with me!" Then she told me, "The Lord takes care of me!"…and finally, after a quiet pause, "I'm so damn lonely. I miss my kids. They should be with their mother!"

If Jude's heart weren't broken anymore, mine was finally beginning to crack.

Session Fifty-Nine

Over the past week Red had thrown a temper tantrum and punched some holes in Jude's wall before Bobby threw him out. Paul was concerned that Jude had been frightened and wanted me to check her out about it. She informed me that she was not frightened by Red's behavior and that Paul, who had shown concern, was still an "Asshole."

She also disclosed that Bobby had asked her to fire Paul as a support worker. It looked like Bobby's behavior was destined to put him in more trouble with the law and the authorities responsible for his mother's welfare. Jude told me again and again, as we talked about Bobby's troubles, "I miss my special Angels!"

She proudly showed me a book on Woody Guthrie that Paul had given her back after she fired him. I found it fascinating and was pouring over it during our session. This irritated her and she pursued me to light her fire when my attention strayed to the book.

Soon after I lit her cigarette, Paul called to apologize. Jude's hands shook, not danced, when she talked to him showing great emotion. She called him "Asshole" three or four times then slipped and called him "Sweetie." I could not see her staying mad at him for long.

Bobby, who was already on probation, for another matter, was scheduled to have a probation meeting later in the day. Jude asked me to attend and I promised her I would be there.

Probation Meeting

At the meeting Jude was very nervous and kept repeating, for all to hear, "I miss my Angel kids!" The meeting, which was attended by an assortment of well-meaning health professionals and representatives from Youth Services and Probation, was designed to be as benign and helpful as possible.

Jude disregarded the good will and saw those attending, with the exception of myself, as enemies who were bent on taking her son from her. Consequently she lied about Bobby's illicit visits to her house, and acted like a woman who had her heart ripped out. It was almost comical, but she wouldn't straighten up no matter how I tried to signal her to cut the act. Though the rest of the table seemed to take her at face value, I got the impression that Bobby was on a one-way street to jail.

Session Sixty

Bobby must have still been exerting his influence on Jude for she immediately hit me up for money as soon as I arrived at her house. When I asked, she candidly told me that it was for Bobby.

Jude's review of the meeting with probation was succinctly summed up in one terse phrase: "The Shits!" She would not admit that Bobby had any responsibility for his wrong doing—either in the past which got him on probation, or the present which revealed him breaking the law and irresponsibly exploiting her own vulnerable situation.

As much as Jude denied fearing Bobby and his friends, she had barricaded her back door with furniture to keep them out of the house because they were "bothering" her. One of Bobby's "friends" had ripped the phone out of the wall on one of his raids, so she could not call for help. I told her I felt things with Bobby were getting out of hand and that he would have to be removed from her life if he didn't get the right help or behave more appropriately. Jude didn't want to hear what I was saying, but trusted that this was not the way I would have chosen to have things work out.

I called the company I worked for and told them of my concern for Jude's safety. My reports, along with Paul's, set a chain of events in motion that eventually resulted in Bobby's removal from the community to a Youth Authority Facility where he would remain until he was stable enough to have a healthier relationship with his mother.

I could have felt like Judas to Jude for encouraging the machinery to have Bobby taken away, but didn't because I told her of my concerns at the risk of her rejecting me. In spite of my stance on Bobby, Jude told me—amidst a chorus of "I miss my Angel kids!"…"They got no right to take my kids from me!"

I would have liked to have brought Jude to a place where she didn't need to constantly grieve the loss of her children, but did feel that her grief was diminishing closer to the point where she could handle it without my help.

Accordingly I prepared her to stop therapy with me in one month. She said she was ready and that her heart was "Okay." Then we looked at a childhood picture of Bobby in *big* cowboy boots. I asked whose boots they were and Jude answered, "Brent's." She said this so completely without rancor that I knew she was almost ready to go it alone.

Session Sixty-One

Jude's spirits were very high coming off the Christmas holidays and the joy of many visits with Jamie. I was thrilled to hear that Mara brought Jamie over with presents and cards, and even more thrilled to hear that *Jude had spontaneously hugged and thanked her for taking such good care of her boy.*

Bobby was still free and visiting often. He had put sheets over the windows so that "bad people couldn't look in." He had also fixed the splintered back door that his "friends" had damaged when they broke in to steal from Jude.

Jude told me that she had been going out to a local hotel to panhandle money for her son. As depraved as this may have sounded, I was glad that she had found a way, in her limited world, to provide for her child's needs.

She ended the session by telling me that she was still very mad at Paul and that he was an "Asshole—thank you God he is gone!"

Session Sixty-Two (Final)

As I arrived for our final session, I found Jude entertaining a man who introduced himself as a friend of Sandy's. He stayed around a few minutes and left the house.

This situation proved that you can never control what is going to happen, even at a session as sacred as a final one after a year and a half of intensive counseling. Jude was sad to let me go and told me that I had "cured" her, implying that she didn't need me anymore.

I presented her with a goodbye present of some polished stones for the medicine bag she wore around her neck. She was touched and moved on to tell me that her court date had been pushed back to April 30. She was hoping for lots of money.

Then she got up and showed me the food in her refrigerator. There she had *Half and Half* for my coffee and butter for piecrust. She was excited about baking a pie with her home care workers.

While I was there a friend called. She told this friend that she was with her counselor "Sol" and would see her later. I noticed that she referred to me on the phone, more than once, as "Sol" and wondered if, or for how long, I would be remembered as "Santa."

Jude talked about being a grandmother some day and told me, (like I didn't know) "I love kids!" During our session she did not utter one word about missing her children. All in all I felt I was leaving her in pretty good shape.

Afterword

I saw Jude only three times in the year since our final session. The first was a quick glance as I drove by her house in the summer. At that time I saw her sitting on her front porch in the sun. I projected happiness and contentment into that moment and have heard no news from my colleagues or anyone else to disprove my projection.

I was made aware, later in the year, that she settled her lawsuit out of court, for considerably less than 950 million dollars—though no one, to my knowledge, had told her how much she had received. She only knows that it is over and that she has enough money to cover the cost of her needs for the rest of her life. So much for dreams of therapeutic ranches.

The second time I saw Jude was several weeks after I glimpsed her on the porch. I spontaneously decided to drop by unannounced after an appointment with another client in her neighborhood. Jude had re-hired Sandy, who was there to pick her up for a therapeutic riding appointment. They were just leaving when I intercepted them in the front yard.

Jude was pleased to see me and dragged me into the house to show me her new furniture. I was relieved to see that the sagging couch and dangerous chair had been replaced with a sturdy plush living room set. The house looked clean and Jude pranced around quickly showing me new additions to the shrine and pictures of her children. Sandy interrupted us hustling Jude out to the car so that they could keep their riding appointment and I vowed to make my next visit on a more formal basis in order to be guaranteed more time together. Nevertheless, I was heartened by what I saw and looked forward to a future visit.

The third time I saw Jude I called her beforehand and made a solid date. When I arrived, she took me into the house which did *not* smell of cigarette smoke as I had known it to in the past. Had she stopped smoking? I couldn't believe it! When I asked, she said she had cut way down and only smoked outside the house.

Telling me about her new smoking habits was the farthest thing from Jude's mind and she dragged me over to the shrine to show me new school pictures of Jamie. She was also beside herself with delight and relief over a letter she had just received from one of her daughters, offering the reunion that I promised would be the result of shedding her bitterness.

The letter was that of a thoughtful and articulate teenager who was preparing to meet her estranged mother after many years of painful separation. It seemed congruent that Jude's daughter was becoming as loving and soulful as her mother and I pointed out that there's no underestimating the power of love. Jude grew quiet and pointed me in the direction of the kitchen to get coffee before we both started to cry.

Jude was very animated throughout our visit. Her Huntington's Chorea was still very evident. At the end of my stay I found myself worn out through the exertion of matching her energy. I guess, after a nine-month hiatus, I was out of shape for her kind of dancing.

The whole time I was with her she did not once say, "I sure miss my Angel kids!"

> *Every therapist desires the fruits of his or her labors to create fertile ground for fur-*
> *ther positive unfolding in a client's life. I know that I have no control over the*
> *future, Jude's or mine, but pray that she will continue to transform the momentum*
> *of our relationship into the fulfillment of her most cherished dreams.*

PART II

A Guide to Rehabilitation Counseling

"The fire must be coaxed out of the unwilling wood—coaxed and nursed. Haste, violence of motion rather than strength, continuity and rhythm will accomplish nothing, nor will indifference, lassitude, or a moment's let-up…patience, perseverance, and delicate control were precisely the requisite qualities."

—**Theodora Krober**, Ishi in two worlds 1961

Introduction

Rehabilitation: from the Latin re + habere, which translates to "back" + "have" or to "have back".

As you can see from the story you have just read, your job as a rehabilitation counselor is to help your client "have back" an image of himself or herself as a whole and healthy person. This is a complex and subtle process that relies, in part, on intelligent, artful, and professional utilization of counseling attitudes and skills. PART II is written to help you better understand how these attitudes and skills were focused and practiced in the story of Jude's rehabilitation and provides guidance that is applicable to all counseling situations.

Chapter 1
The Structure and Nature of Teamwork

THE FORMAL STRUCTURE OF TEAMWORK

It is indicative of the underlying value we place on maintaining a healthy society that the formal responsibility and structure provided to help a person gain his or her life back, after injury, is mostly maintained by community in one form or another. This form varies from culture to culture, country to country, state to state, and community to community. The rehabilitation counselor's role in this structure is supported, along with others, by institutions set up to provide services to the disabled. These institutions include, among others, insurance companies, governmental agencies, rehabilitation hospitals, services and clinics (both profit and non-profit), support groups, churches, tribal councils, and outreach groups. In relation to Jude's story I can only describe the formal structure, which funded my relationship with her rehabilitation.

It was as follows:

Any motor vehicle driven on public roads in British Columbia has to be licensed and insured by the Insurance Corporation of British Columbia for legal use in the province. This insurance does not only cover the vehicle and its driver but all persons involved in an accident with an insured vehicle including passengers, operators, pedestrians, and anyone injured by an insured vehicle. The extent of no-fault coverage is for rehabilitation only and provides $150,000 of funds for verified injuries until a legal claim with the company is settled. This money is administered through a rehabilitation department staffed by professionals responsible for the coordination of services and case management. All of Jude's rehabilitation needs, including my salary, the salaries of home care workers Paul, Sandy and Mary, and any health needs and specialized support not covered by provincial healthcare, were covered by these funds and coordinated through the insurance company's case manager(s). Other needs were met through advances from her lawyer, social services, and non-profit groups such as the Salvation Army and local brain injury societies.

Falling through the cracks

Some injuries cannot be verified by medical testing, regardless of clinically recorded debilitating symptoms. Clients with these symptoms, who are bonafide victims of motor vehicle accidents in British Columbia, are not eligible for the no-fault insurance mentioned above. In these cases rehabilitation funds are covered by family or advanced by lawyers against anticipated rewards from legal claims. Support of this nature is often unreliable and hard won, for good rehabilitation services are expensive and not usually within the reach of most families and legal advances.

Knowing your client's support system

As a rehabilitation counselor it was imperative that I clearly understood the resources and boundaries of Jude's support system. This understanding came from studying her case, information sessions offered by the insurance company, and a good collegial relationship with her case manager(s).

It is important to learn whatever is available about the structure that supports your relationship with an individual client, in order to be able to concentrate your full energies upon your work as a counselor. The agencies that support your work often provide the support of other rehabilitation professionals and you will find yourself a member of a team that is defined by the nature of your client's injuries and support requirements.

The Nature of Teamwork

Restoring a self-image inevitably varies from client to client for each injury, or combination of injuries, creates a unique response in an individual. Due to the fact that human beings have physical, social, familial, and spiritual relationships, rehabilitation must take place in a climate of cooperation with members of a multi-faceted team that is qualified to help a client come back to healthy function in all these worlds.

The collegial relationship

In my opinion any person, being, or thing your client elects to be of influence in his or her world is a colleague worth cultivating. Colleagues are vital links to the laws of your client's universe and are available, in varying degrees, for you to consult in your quest to create and facilitate the most positive and effective path to rehabilitation.

You are not alone

As a counselor it is easy to be lulled into thinking that your clinical work exists in the rarified Rogerian environment of a one-to-one realm enhanced by empathy, undivided attention, and unconditional positive regard. This may be true in the privacy of therapy, but the fruit of therapeutic progress is best realized, through teamwork and consultation with colleagues in respectful and professional collegial relationships, *paying meticulous attention to your client's release of confidentiality.*

THE FORGOTTEN COLLEAGUES

Your client

Your client is the most important and often most forgotten colleague in the rehabilitation process. He or she must be consulted in all aspects of rehabilitation to ensure that therapeutic efforts find receptive ground. This consultation must be undertaken regardless of limited ability to communicate or seeming inability to understand. Constant client consultation is an essential task that requires patience, sensitivity and compassion—and there is no one more qualified than you, the counselor, to make sure it gets done. It is one of your most important responsibilities to keep your client first in the consultation process and help others do so through example and education.

Colleagues not present

Some forgotten colleagues cannot be present to consult in person, because they have died or left your client's life for one reason or another. These "missing" members are valuable consultants and can be reached through employing such counseling tools as role-playing and creative reminiscence. Don't forget that their past input still influences your client. They can be reawakened and consulted as colleagues when brought to life through your empathy and skills.

Chapter 2
Colleagues of Physical Relationships

Colleagues of physical relationships include doctors, health professionals and technicians, nurses, specialists, medical support workers, physiotherapists, and alternative health practitioners. Some of these colleagues may view counselors as less important or less effective members of the rehabilitation team because the work of counseling does not always produce effects that are visible to them. Do not be offended by sometimes uneducated attitudes about your profession, but look upon your relationship with these colleagues as an opportunity to learn from their expertise and, in turn, teach them about what you do and how you can work together.

DOCTORS

Your client's doctor is one of your most important references, as he or she holds the key to influential therapies that can encourage positive responses from your client through direct or indirect medical treatment.

Learning from medical records

Among the cause and effect language of medical records are pearls of information that can help you better understand your client's responses to pre- and post-injury circumstances. This makes your client's doctor a potential ally in the unfolding and maintenance of therapeutic progress. Therefore I strongly recommend that you consult your client's doctor or doctors. Don't forget that your observations may prove extremely useful to the doctor and be of help in his or her provision of vital health care.

HEALTH PROFESSIONALS AND TECHNICIANS

Health professionals and providers, such as dentists, optometrists/opticians, and medical technicians, provide services and support that can change your client's state of mind and self-image through alleviating pain, sharpening senses, and enhancing the ability to enjoy life. They also have the qualifications to diagnose, treat, and refer your client to specialists for progressively debilitating conditions that threaten essential health and progress in therapy. It is to your advantage to coordinate efforts with these colleagues, and encourage cooperation with treatments that might seem hopeless or disagreeable. Don't forget that it is part of your job, as a counselor, to nurture and create the position of a respected and knowledgeable colleague who has earned your client's ear. If this is achieved, other professionals and colleagues will usually acknowledge this role and welcome your consultation.

SPECIALISTS

Specialists come in as many forms as there are specific medical problems to treat. Their focused experience in caring for other patients afflicted with your client's specific medical problem makes them a tremendous resource in the understanding of disease related behaviors.

It is wise to suspend your judgments, if any, of the medical profession and put yourself at the tutelage of specialists, as they are often driven by enthusiasm for their field of expertise and have great compassion for their patients. It is also my experience that they see the counselor as an ally and are willing to consult and share their knowledge in the further understanding and service of their patients.

INSTITUTIONAL NURSES

If your client has had a connection with a hospital, rehabilitation institution, or doctor's office, he or she will have relationships with nurses who are trained and experienced in acute or extended rehabilitation care. All of these relationships are, by necessity, both practical and intimate. It is good to remember that these professionals may hold your client's trust as they often make themselves available on a deep and personal level. If this is the case it is important to encourage and support bonds of positive connection, for they are the very building blocks injured clients must have to reestablish a trusting relationship with the world.

Problems with Health Professionals

On the other hand, a nurse or other health professional may have offended and put off your client through not being able to fully understand or respond to some acute or unspoken need. Be supportive when listening to complaints and careful not to encourage enmity between your client and the caregiver in question. Maintain the attitude of an impartial listener and simply allow your client to respond to feeling mistreated.

Nurses are often responsible for the practical application of a doctor's or specialist's orders. Consequently your ability to communicate clearly and accurately with them and your client can be vital to the successful application of essential medical therapies.

HOME CARE NURSES

Home care nurses have much the same function as institutional nurses but are charged with the responsibility of carrying out their duties in your client's home. This brings them directly into your sphere of work, especially if you choose to see your clients in their place of residence. Accordingly it is to your benefit to coordinate with them, to ensure that your client is getting the fullest benefit of his or her prescribed medical treatment.

Home care nurses tend to create the same intimate relationships with their patients as other nurses, and can provide vital and immediate relationships for your client to process with you in therapy. Remember to ask for and respect your client's needs for confidentiality and privacy, if you end up counseling him or her for any relationship problems with home care nurses or other workers.

MEDICAL SUPPORT WORKERS

Medical support workers are non-medical staff working in a medical environment, and can provide the earliest post-traumatic experience your client has with his or her peer group. What these workers may lack in medical training is often highly compensated for by natural empathy, compassion, and common sense. As there is no substitute for kindness, many of your client's most positive and memorable post-injury relationships are with some of the people who have taken good care of his or her basic needs of hygiene, transportation and recreation.

Support workers as a resource

Medical support workers can give you some of the most unbiased information about the physical and mental state of your client during various stages of recovery in and out of institutions. This is because they are just there to be helpful and have no particular treatment bias or point to prove. Therefore it is in your client's best interest for you to build solid relationships, and keep open lines of communication with the people who care for his or her immediate one-on-one needs.

PHYSIOTHERAPISTS

Physiotherapists can be a vital link for your client in his or her quest to reestablish mastery of the body. Any ground that you may gain through counseling to recover the mindset and attitude necessary for physical rehabilitation needs to be supported by real knowledge of how the body works. Physiotherapists are trained in the application of this knowledge. They know how to plan and provide a therapeutic program with understanding, and utilize available aids designed to encourage the body's capacity to heal.

The counselor as a go-between

As a counselor you can be privy to your client's unique ideas of how to achieve success in his or her physical rehabilitation program. The physiotherapist needs to know these ideas in order to create the most individually tailored and effective therapy possible. Consequently it becomes your responsibility to help your client communicate all ideas (including negative responses to present treatment) to the physiotherapist in order to facilitate progress in physiotherapy.

ALTERNATIVE HEALTH PRACTITIONERS

We live in a world of infinite influences and choices of action. Therefore not everyone perceives the generation of health and injury in the same manner. This multitude of perceptions has given rise to many schools of health and healing. Most are driven by the spiritual and scientific understandings of the cultures that spawned them and all, in my opinion, are valid in the context of their creation.

Supporting your client's world view

I believe that it is your job, as a counselor, to discover and honor your client's essential view of the world, so that you can help create and advocate for treatment that best encourages his or her most natural healing process. Many clients hold beliefs that direct them to look outside the usual channels of Western medicine for therapeutic results. If this is so, it follows that it is also your job, as a counselor, to help them explore the efficacy of these beliefs.

Alternative versus Western medicine

Due to the fact that most institutions set up to support rehabilitation in North America were created through the Western medical profession, all therapies outside of that model are considered "alternative"—and often are not supported. This creates a difficulty for the client who believes that the relief for his or her problem(s) lies in alternative therapies.

As a rehabilitation counselor you can do no more than help your client research the availability of therapies that he or she may think are beneficial. It is also your responsibility to consult and coordinate your efforts with chosen and approved alternative health providers as you would with members of the more traditional medical profession.

Chapter 3
Colleagues of Social Relationships

Colleagues of social relationships include any and all that are concerned with your client's relationship to the world of others. These may be social workers, occupational therapists, rehabilitation coordinators, vocational counselors/job coaches, mental health professionals (including psychologists and counselors), home care and support workers, lawyers, law enforcement personnel, school staff and officials, support groups/drop-ins, friends, and acquaintances. All members of this long and widely varied list should be considered valuable and consulted with regard to their involvement and specific importance to your client.

SOCIAL WORKERS

Some social workers are employed by hospitals, government, and other institutions to connect your client with resources that support and sustain his or her rehabilitation. This service includes access to confidential records, reports and recommendations for further treatment. Though you may never meet the social worker you can learn a tremendous amount about your client's rehabilitation needs from his or her reports. These confidential records are your link to the observations and expertise of various professionals involved in the acute or extended care of your client after injury.

Reading records and reports

Be careful, when you read reports, to look out for language that negatively judges, objectifies, or limits your client's potential. This negative language more often reflects the viewpoint of the person who writes it than it reflects your client. Remember that your client's *response* to trauma, disability, and treatment creates the only viable reality within which the establishment of positive change can take place. It can also be beneficial and therapeutic to discuss records and treatment plans with your client, as he or she will let you know what is working and what is not. Sometimes, with your client's permission, you can go back to the authors of the reports and consult with them about your client's positive or negative responses to their treatment plans.

Survival needs

If your client has lost the ability to make a living through a disability and does not have family funds, independent wealth, or eligibility for compensation through his or her employer, he or she will most likely seek support through a government provided disability or welfare agency. In most cases the professional responsible for linking your client to publicly funded resources is a social worker. These resources simply translate to the basics of food, shelter, clothing and protection, and are crucial to your client's well-being and ability to rehabilitate. In the provision of this service the social worker will come to know your client and his or her family very well, as the process of connection to resources depends upon a clear knowledge of your client's needs and familial responsibilities.

The social worker as counselor

Social workers are trained, like counselors, in the art and science of interview, and work to draw out and discover your client's remaining abilities and inclinations in order to ensure workable and sustainable connections to resources. Once again it is your responsibility, as a counselor, to help your client work with the social worker. It is also your responsibility to help the social worker better understand your client.

Your responsibilities to the social worker

It is not out of line for you to be forthright in your suggestions and criticism if you believe that the therapeutic progress or rights of your client are being compromised by the social worker or anyone else. In fact, if you perceive or learn that the safety of your client, or members of his or her family (especially minors) is seriously threatened, it is your duty, after careful study and consideration, to report your observations to the social worker (or child protection worker). He or she is the link to resources that are responsible for your client's protection.

In cases of abuse or harm to minors or threats of bodily harm to the client or others, it is your legal duty (at least in British Columbia) to report your findings to authorities, including social workers, without respect for client confidentiality.

Again, I strongly caution you to carefully research and verify your suspicions concerning harm and abuse *before reporting*, unless the facts are indisputable, as reporting false or misinformed allegations can backfire and seriously harm the welfare of your client, his or her family, or yourself.

OCCUPATIONAL THERAPISTS

I find the title of occupational therapist somewhat misleading because, in my experience, these professionals influence and affect more than just the rehabilitation of "occupation." They are responsible for the provision and coordination of therapies and aids that facilitate the return of functional patterns in your client's life.

Occupational therapists in the work place

Occupational therapists are often dually educated in physiotherapy and "occupational" therapy and need to have intimate knowledge of your client's physical and social surroundings. During appropriate phases of rehabilitation they are also responsible for helping your client re-engage in his or her career or workplace. This task includes coordination with past, present, and prospective employers, vocational counselors, and institutions for re-training. Due to the holistic nature of their relationship with your client, occupational therapists are often chosen by providers of rehabilitation funding and programs to provide the role of case manager. In most instances your input, as a counselor, is highly valued and sought after by the occupational therapist, who needs to understand your client's progress in counseling to provide effective therapy and case management. You, as a rehabilitation counselor, also need the occupational therapist's input and consultation, to integrate and coordinate progress in counseling with your client's bid to restore independence and self-sufficiency.

REHABILITATION COORDINATORS

In my work with Jude the most important member of the team was the rehabilitation coordinator. She worked for the rehabilitation department of the insurance company that funded Jude's rehabilitation. Her job included the roles of case manager and social worker, for it was through her that many of Jude's survival and rehabilitation needs were coordinated until Jude's ongoing claim against the insurance company was settled. I also reported directly to her on our progress in counseling, and advocated for what I believed to be beneficial changes in the provision of services for my client.

As the rehabilitation coordinator was the most important professional in our world, it was of ultimate importance to maintain a candid and respectful relationship with her. She was also a link to the administrative ear in my attempts to influence company policy that I felt was detrimental to our progress.

VOCATIONAL COUNSELORS/JOB COACHES/ SPECIALISTS

Each one of these professionals comes with a different level of expertise, education, and experience. Most are specially trained counselors and job coaches while others can be highly skilled and specialized psychologists.

Vocational Counselors

Specifically trained vocational counselors are able to help your client contemplate the possibility of resuming an old career or re-train and engage in the search for a new one. They use many counseling skills in their work and it can be said that the focus on vocation combined with counseling is an especially potent and useful part of the rehabilitation process. This is because loss of career through disability directly threatens survival and is extremely devastating to self-image.

It is no wonder that there is an overlap of your work with the career counselor's. This does not have to be a point of confusion or competition, but rather an opportunity for invaluable collaboration and consultation. The sharing of your client's progress in counseling can help the vocational therapist pace the process of career search or reengagement to readiness for change.

Job coaches

Job coaches carry out the plans of vocational counselors and spend a lot of one-on-one time with your client helping him or her set up and follow the prescription for vocational exploration or re-training. They are not necessarily educated in counseling and, like other helpers, can be extremely effective, or not, depending on their innate compassion and ability to relate to your client. It is to your advantage to consult with them about your client's progress so that you can help them be more understanding and effective in their work.

OTHER VOCATIONAL SPECIALISTS

Professionals such as some neuropsychologists specialize in the vocational field. Their main focus is in rehabilitation from brain injury and they can provide your brain injured client with training and career guidance that is exactly tailored to his or her specific rehabilitation needs. These highly trained professionals use the investigative instruments of their profession to provide detailed and effective plans and support systems in preparation for the world of work. They often draw distinct boundaries around their role and do not see themselves as counselors but skilled scientists and facilitators at the service of your client's rehabilitation team. Count yourself lucky if you have one of these specialists on your team and by all means consult him or her whenever possible.

MENTAL HEALTH PROFESSIONALS AND SPECIALISTS

As a counselor you may or may not be the only mental health professional on your client's rehabilitation team. Others can include the social worker, vocational professional, or case manager, and previous or concurrent psychologists and counselors.

Counselors and psychologists

Consultation with other counselors and psychologists, past or present, can give you a great amount of new insight, for each therapist has his or her unique and educated way of looking at your client's case. Other viewpoints, especially those of psychologists who specialize in sleep, sexual, speech or neurological disorders, are as useful to your understanding of your client as those of medical specialists. Like medical specialists, they are often passionate and deeply knowledgeable about their fields and can help your client address specific problems related to his or her disability.

Addictions counselors

Another specialist who may be very helpful to consult and possibly refer to is an addictions counselor. Addictions counselors are specially trained to treat addictions which can seriously impede your client's progress. These workers' specialized approach may be closely related to yours, in terms of counseling skills and attitudes, but focuses on boundaries that need to be maintained in the presence of a debilitating addiction.

Groups

Some mental health professionals also provide group sessions that your client may attend, for conditions including anger management, grief, and drug and alcohol addiction. You might not be able to meet with group leaders as colleagues, but it is important to study their handouts and discuss with your client what he or she has learned from the group or workshop experience. Sometimes your client will need to process his or her responses to group relationships or events in therapy with you. In this manner you are including the group experience itself as an influential member of your rehabilitation team.

HOME CARE AND SUPPORT WORKERS

Home care and support workers are your client's concrete link to the provision of many important rehabilitation needs, including help with activities of daily living and some prescribed treatments. They literally translate treatment plans into action and are responsible for assuring that your client makes, keeps, and gets to appointments and therapies. Aside from these vital functions, they often provide real friendship that is both supportive and therapeutic, as they usually see your client on a frequent basis. These team members are among your most important and rewarding colleagues to consult in order to monitor the progress of your therapies and those of others. As with other colleagues, their knowledge and practice of appropriate boundaries may be problematic, but can be turned to the benefit of your counseling process through consultation.

LAWYERS

Lawyers come with many specialties and are all committed to an adversarial system of law. The ones you will most likely have contact with, as a rehabilitation counselor, are personal injury lawyers who specialize in helping people who have been disabled gain rewards from insurance companies created to compensate them for injury. So stated, a troubling question occurs to me: Why must there be lawyers to advocate and demand compensation for injury from the very companies created to provide compensation? The answer to this question lies in the adversarial nature and structure of tort law. Insurance companies usually do make good on their commitment to the insured and also have the right to carefully examine and quantify the level of disablement from claims against them. This is not necessarily a declaration of war, between the disabled and the insurance company, but usually is experienced as one, before and during the time a settlement is achieved. Some of your clients may be involved in just such a process, and hopefully will have involved a lawyer to advocate for and help them through it.

The lawyer as an ally

The good news is that the personal injury lawyer is on your client's side in the perceived battle for fair settlement of a disability claim. This makes him or her an ally and team member worth cultivating. A creative personal injury lawyer can work with case managers to uncover sources of funding for rehabilitation when other channels have been blocked or dried up. Don't forget that it is to your client's benefit to consult with his or her lawyer because information you share can help quantify disability in the battle to win a fair settlement from an insurance company.

LAW ENFORCEMENT PERSONNEL

Your client can find himself or herself involved with law enforcement personnel for at least two reasons: He or she may either need their protection, or be perceived as someone from whom the public needs protection. In both cases you want an open line of communication with law enforcement personnel, as you are the professional most responsible for your client's emotional attitude and well being. Do not be intimidated by law enforcement personnel. They are often inclined to see you as a member of their team if you approach them with respect and collegiality.

When your client needs protection

If your client needs the protection of the law, you need to be able to assess the danger and help him or her make the decision whether or not to ask for help. You also need to be able to support your client's dealing with the consequences of decisions made by the justice system. In both these situations you can find some law enforcement personnel supportive and compassionate consultants.

When your client is perceived as a threat

When it is your client who is perceived to be a threat to the community, consultation is vital, because some behaviors that come with disability need to be re-interpreted as non-threatening to those who don't understand their source. You also need to be able to help your client through the horror of being falsely accused, and can act as a translator between well meaning but misinformed parties.

If your client has broken the law it is your responsibility to help him or her understand and process the consequences of his or her actions. It is also your responsibility to help ensure that your client receives the most understanding and humane treatment possible from law enforcement personnel and agencies.

SCHOOL STAFF AND OFFICIALS

School staff and officials are usually receptive to counselor input because of their respect for the profession of counseling. Don't forget that these institutions usually have a counselor on staff who will solicit your input, if needed, about a disabled client's particular state or needs. These counselors, and other staff, are educated to solve problems and, in my experience, defer to your expertise if you keep within the bounds of your position as a visiting consultant in their institution. Good relations with school staff and personnel are very important if your client is already a student or in the process of re-educating or training, because these activities comprise one of the most crucial parts of his or her bid for independence and a return to the world.

NON-PROFIT SOCIETIES, SUPPORT GROUPS AND DROP-INS

Non-profit societies, support groups, and drop-in situations are created to help survivors of a particular disability by providing links to numerous resources, including support groups and drop-in situations. Professionals and survivors of the disability usually staff these societies. The professionals are most frequently social workers, occupational therapists, case managers, counselors, and/or nurses. You can learn a great deal from these professionals because they have specific experience helping people who share your client's specific disability and problems. You can also gain information from them about resources and potential solutions for problems. Your consultation with professional members of disability organizations is usually welcome as these professionals are highly dedicated to increasing public and professional awareness of a particular disability. They are also often eager to gain professional allies and spread the word about their organizations and its activities. This makes them valuable colleagues who can directly help develop an acceptable peer group for your client.

Support groups

Non-professional members of support groups (i.e., survivors) can develop real life relationships with your client as peers, and bring vivid and relevant material to the work of counseling as you help your client celebrate, practice, or process the re-experiencing of collateral relationships. Your client may not feel comfortable with your consultation of these colleagues, but it is good for you to enjoy a passing level of acquaintance with them, if possible, so you can more accurately reference and reflect your client's comments or concerns about them.

Friends

Friends are often a source of emotional connection or distress. This depends on whether they relate to your client in a supportive and natural manner.

Present friends

It is to your advantage to support your client's relationships with his or her friends. Be especially careful to check in often with your client regarding confidentiality and stay within the boundary of a helping professional whose interest is only that of therapeutic rehabilitation.

Lost friends

Your client may report the loss of friends who knew him or her before disablement—how they "dropped away" or "disappeared." These friends (or non-friends) can be a source of emotional pain as they reflect the great change and loss (disablement) in your client's life which resulted in abandonment. Your client will automatically see himself or herself as negatively changed from "before" and feel unworthy of friendship. This is a huge blow to the self-image and is softened if the lost friend unaccountably reappears or grows back. Friends who have abandoned your client are not to be considered colleagues until they do come back and reestablish contact. If and when they do, they will usually bring reflections of strengths in your client's personality that you need to be aware of in order to draw out a new and healthy self-image.

Acquaintances

Acquaintances of your client may or may not be viable colleagues depending upon the frequency of contact and health of relationship. Acquaintances can include store clerks, restaurant staff, public service providers, or anyone else your client meets outside of his or her circle of friends, family, health professionals, therapists, and support workers. Neighbors and passers-by often fit in the category of acquaintances. The presence of these peripheral members of the team is minor but can provide material for helping your client process, in session, his or her contacts with society. As a counselor, you will come to know some of your client's acquaintances through reports or anecdotes about them, and you may also brush shoulders with them when you accompany your client on daily walks, outings, or recreational expeditions. It is important to guard your client's confidentiality in these particular contacts by letting your client introduce you first, if he or she wishes, or introducing yourself as a "friend" if asked.

Chapter 4
Family

Nobody except family knows your client like family—and nobody, except your client, is closer to his or her disability than family. This is because family is the most intimate and hopeful of all relationships. Intimate in physical, emotional, and spiritual response, and hopeful in the fulfillment of dreams, promises and vows. Clients are always someone's children and can be spouses/partners, siblings, and parents. They are connected in these roles by deep bonds of love, responsibility and duty. When trauma and disability affect the status of any member of the constellation of familial relationships, all members respond in keeping with the special conditions of their connection. This makes them potentially invaluable and sometimes problematic colleagues.

PARENTS

Children are created with the expectation that they will out-live and possibly be more successful than their parents. This is the unwritten rule of parenthood and informs the heart and soul of every parent. When a child is traumatized or seriously injured an essential part of a parent's worldview is threatened. When a child is disabled or compromised as a result of trauma or injury there is virtually no place for this experience in the parent's world, and he or she suffers a complete or partial breakdown of faith. In my mind this makes all parents, regardless of their response, exempt from judgment and worthy of your greatest compassion.

In the face of a child's disablement, some parents are devastated and disabled through extreme grief and expenditure of emotion. Others can put on a brave face and seemingly kick into action, but it is wise to keep in mind that their efforts, though brave, may be half hearted at best. As a counselor you will hear your client's version of his or her relationship with parents and response to their hopes, dreams, and expectations. This information can help you understand, encourage, and guide him or her to internal strengths inherited from that relationship. In this manner, parents become colleagues of the past whose vital influence is still great, but limited to your client's ability to integrate their memory. There is often a great amount of grieving that goes along with the exploration of these memories, as your client may be experiencing the tremendous loss of not being able to live up to parents' expectations through his or her disablement. It is your job to help your client acknowledge all of his or her losses and grieve them fully.

If your client is fortunate enough to have living parent(s) who are willing to consult and visit with you, then you have the opportunity to help them grieve so that they can translate their love into actions that further your client's healing and rehabilitation. Some parents are difficult to work with as they justifiably claim that they know what is right for your client. They may not agree with you and other members of the rehabilitation team. The key to working with parents is to approach them with the greatest respect for their position in your client's life and remember that, no matter what anyone may say, *they always want the best for their children.*

SPOUSES AND PARTNERS

Adult clients are often married or have a live-in partner. These relationships are built on the expectation of realizing ideals inherent in the formal or informal vows of marriage and partnering. It is difficult enough to meet these expectations under the normal circumstances of life, and much more challenging when one member of a relationship is disabled through trauma or injury. Husbands, wives, and partners individually respond to the disabilities of their mates with unique strengths and weaknesses. Some may abandon the disabled mate because their grief is too great to bear in the presence of the broken promise of their future, while others will respond to their mate's increased need by sacrificing all to the recreation of that promise through involvement in the rehabilitation process.

Spouses and partners can also help you verify your client's stories about him or herself so that you can be a more effective guide through the process of reminiscence and restoration of self-image.

Ex-partners

A breakdown of relations between your client and his or her ex-mate is common if the relationship was under stress at the time of your client's disablement. Though sometimes difficult to process in the presence of the stress of trauma and its aftermath, the response to a failed relationship can provide rich material about personal expectations for performance under stress. This can add to your knowledge of how your client may respond to the highs and lows of the rehabilitative process. In this manner spouses and partners become valuable consultants whether they are present or not.

SIBLINGS

Siblings make great team members and are often willing to consult and participate in your client's rehabilitation, depending on their willingness, availability, and health. The state of your client's past and present relationship with his or her siblings also determines whether or not they can become useful and practical colleagues.

Age and position in the family influence your client's relationship with his or her brother or sister. The characteristics of this relationship are usually formed by the time of disablement.

Older siblings

Older siblings naturally tend to be protective of their younger brothers or sisters. They may try to control or manipulate the rehabilitation process to make sure your client is getting the best care. This can be either a help or hindrance in the carrying out of a rehabilitation program depending on agreement or disagreement with prescribed therapies. It is good to consult older siblings for, as with parents, you can usually count on them to have your client's best interests at heart. They also have known your client longer than you have and can be a valuable source of information about his or her strengths, weaknesses, and personality traits.

Younger siblings

Younger siblings have enjoyed the protection of your client as an older sibling and role model, and may be distressed by the unwanted responsibility of being pressed into service to care for their disabled older brother or sister. It is important to consider their new position in the family when consulting, and be compassionate in your communication with them. Your client may also express great distress at not being able to relate to a younger brother or sister in a more competent and protective manner. This distress is usually a manifestation of the grief that comes from losing a cherished position in the family, and can be addressed through acknowledging and grieving this particular loss with your client.

Siblings and parents

Siblings often side with parents in resisting what they consider to be treatment that is ignorant of the family's values and unique relationships. The resistance of this united block can create a serious conflict for the counselor who believes that his or her primary alliance is with the client and is dedicated to supporting the rehabilitation team. This conflict can be resolved if you clarify to siblings and family that you value their input and truly consider them an important part of the rehabilitation team. One way of including family is to nurture an open relationship with them and advocate for regular team meetings that include your client and his or her family.

CHILDREN

From the beginning, the world of the parent becomes the world of the child. The drive to provide the needs of survival, protection, and love develops and becomes relatively self-sustaining—but doesn't discriminate these needs as separate. When your client is a parent, he or she is as fully committed to providing the world for his or her child as the child is dependent upon its provision. When this ability to provide is interrupted by trauma and injury, both parent and child are deeply affected. The parent loses a large part of his or her reason for existence and the child experiences the loss of a known and seemingly secure world. A child's dependence usually correlates to age but can also depend on health, family history, life experience, and circumstances.

The child as colleague

When you relate to your client's child as a colleague it is important to know and understand his or her level of dependence on your client. Each level of dependence needs to be responded to individually with counseling skills and attitudes to match age and emotional maturity.

Resistance from the child

Some children tend to block rehabilitative efforts which they perceive to further threaten their relationships with a parent. Even though this is troublesome, it is a valid response from a most valuable colleague and can give you insight into the historical nature of the relationship that exists between your client and his or her child.

Chapter 5
Colleagues of Spiritual
Relationships

Colleagues of spiritual relationships are not limited to human beings. They can be anyone or anything that strengthens your client's flow of life energy and encourages a positive response in the healing process. Biological colleagues include humans, animals, plants, and any living phenomena. Other colleagues include the creative processes of art, music, dance and writing. Still others include the spiritual expression and disciplines of chanting, prayer, meditation, visualization and ritual. Some clients may believe they are in contact with their ancestors, dead teachers, Jesus, Buddha, or even God.

Consulting spiritual colleagues demands that you set aside your own prejudices and judgments in favor of accepting your client's most sacred truths.

SPIRITUAL LEADERS/COUNSELORS

Spiritual leaders or counselors come in as many forms as there are religious or spiritual groups to lead or work through. The most common of these colleagues, in North America, are priests, ministers, rabbis, medicine men/women, gurus, spiritual guides/teachers/counselors, and their Buddhist, Islamic, and Hindu, counterparts. This roster is probably much more detailed and varied than I have listed, due to the multicultural nature of most modern societies.

Specific religions

If your client is receiving or has received help through a specific religion, find out as much as you can about how he or she relates to its beliefs and practices. It is important that you respond to your client's request to meet with the colleagues responsible for his or her spiritual exploration, for they may be best able to help you understand how to restore the faith and hope that have been threatened or lost through trauma and disability. Consulting with accepted spiritual colleagues, if possible, can also give you the credibility to work with family who believe that healing can only come through their traditional spiritual channels.

ANIMALS, PLANTS AND NATURE

Some clients have spiritual relationships with non-human companions. Most choose animals, both domestic and exotic, while others commune best with plants and nature. It is important to understand and value these relationships for they can directly and positively influence your client's response to being alive. This response is the foundation upon which all healing is dependent for success.

Get to know your client's animals, plants and favorite places in nature through direct experience, stories, reminiscence, keepsakes, photographs, or your shared experience as an empathetic human being.

CREATIVE PROCESSES

Creative processes and their products are not usually considered animate objects, but they provide a real channel for living energy. Consequently art, music, writing, and dance can be considered viable spiritual colleagues if your client is, or has been, actively involved as a creator or appreciator. His or her level of participation in a chosen creative act can be compromised by disability, which will most probably bring up grief over lost abilities. It is your job as a counselor to help your client through his or her response to these losses, and acknowledge and encourage realistic interests in old or newly acquired creative relationships. In this manner you are directly involved in supporting the healing of the spirit as it seeks to find voice through creative endeavor.

Creative teachers and therapists

Your work may bring you in contact with important teachers and therapists who specialize in the creative arts.

It is my experience that most clients are eager to share their artwork and creative triumphs with you. You can enhance your understanding of these artifacts, and their relevance to your therapeutic efforts, through consulting creative teachers and therapists about your client's progress in the chosen discipline.

SPIRITUAL EXPRESSION

Spirituality can find expression in as many forms as there are individuals to express it. It often manifests as a unique combination of learned ritual, and with the deepest response to being alive. This combination is translated into spiritual tools that we automatically employ and summon to help us when we are overwhelmed by trauma and disability.

Spiritual tools

Spiritual tools may include learned and improvised chants, mantras, prayers or rituals that mitigate the impact of negative change. These rituals are important colleagues that you can consult with through listening to and observing your client's response to their employment. They will show you how to encourage and strengthen a positive response to healing from trauma.

COLLEAGUES OF THE PAST AND OTHER WORLDS

Some beings exist outside of our ordinary sphere of perception. We believe and have faith in our connection with them through sacred text, story, vision, and spiritual tradition. The big names in this group are Jesus, Buddha, Mohamed, and (sometimes) God. Other beings include angels, spirit guides (human and animal), ancestors, and family members who have passed on. These entities are most influential, as they are the touchstones and reference points of your client's inner life. Your client's relationship with these entities exists within the private and intimate boundaries of religion, prayer and altered states of consciousness. It is not always readily accessible to you as a counselor—nor is it meant to be. It is, however, your responsibility to honor and validate your client's response to these spiritual connections if you believe that they are positively influencing his or her process of restoration. Therefore it is helpful to learn as much as you can about chosen spiritual colleagues and consult with them through your own abilities of contemplation, observation, and careful study.

Chapter 6
The Attitudes of a Counselor

You may wonder, after reading the descriptions of colleagues in the previous chapters, what special role you play in your client's rehabilitation. What do you do that none of the other members of the team do, and how does this contribute to the physical, social, and spiritual health of your client?

The answer to these questions is shaped by your unique expression as a human being and by your attitudes in the practice of counseling. The attitudes I have chosen to present in this guide are drawn from those of "person centered therapy"—the method of counseling in which I was trained. I have found this method, which is based on the work of Carl Rogers (1951, 1957), to be most resonant with my natural way of being. It is a "process oriented" therapy that derives its utility from the experience of both counselor and client in the therapeutic relationship.

BE YOURSELF

There is nothing more significant in building and maintaining a meaningful relationship with another than the act of being yourself. Your client depends upon you to give honest reflections of his or her state of being. The fact that you are a counselor binds you to respond with therapeutic purpose. In my mind this translates to a *true friendship that is dedicated to positive growth and infused with the attitudes of empathy, unconditional positive regard, and undivided attention* (Rogers, 1957).

EMPATHY

Empathy simply means "in feeling" and is an ability that is not unique to the profession of counseling. It is relatively easy to empathize with something you have had direct experience with, but much more difficult to do so outside of your exact history. The ability to feel with another if you have not shared his or her experience is a foundational attitude of rehabilitation counseling and can be achieved through extrapolation.

Extrapolation

In order to earn credibility as a friend and helping professional you need to be able to empathize with your client's response to trauma and disability. Though you may not have exactly experienced his or her loss, you can look within yourself to find any experience of loss in your life that resembles your client's in any way. If you allow yourself to feel your response to this loss and imagine yourself in your client's situation you can establish a form of empathy that goes a long way toward experiencing your client's response to trauma and disablement.

Be careful not to verbally acknowledge to your client that you "know how it feels." You only know how you felt in a similar situation. You will never know exactly how your client feels, but you can attend to him or her with all the likeness of feeling that you can bring to the moment.

UNCONDITIONAL POSITIVE REGARD

Unconditional positive regard is the act of always seeing another in the most positive light you can create. It is not an act of extrapolation like empathy but a witness to our ability to feel through the heart and realize our highest intention as loving beings. Unconditional positive regard is the true realization of another's potential for positive growth and must be present to motivate a successful therapeutic relationship.

Seeing your client as a child

Relating to someone else with unconditional positive regard can be a challenge if you maintain any negative judgments of that person's past or present behavior. In such cases it is helpful to visualize the other person as a very young child before he or she was capable of willfully negative behavior. The being who was that child is still there to be experienced without judgment as a positive and well intentioned person.

Undivided Attention

Undivided attention is the ability to treat your client as if he or she is the only person on earth within your scope of attention. This type of attention is evidence that you are empathizing and relating with unconditional positive regard.

Maintaining undivided attention

Sometimes undivided attention may be difficult to maintain, if you are fatigued or distracted by your own problems, so it is good to let your client know, without dwelling on details, when you feel your attention might have been compromised by outside circumstances. This type of disclosure is an indication of your consideration and can be therapeutic when your client is taken into your confidence and treated as an equal partner in the counseling relationship. It is important not to forget that you are also vulnerable.

Chapter 7
Dangers of the Profession

The pitfalls of counseling are not overt, as in other dangerous professions, but hidden within your responses to competency, intimacy, and power. Before you choose any course of action that you feel might be dangerous, ask yourself "Is this in the service of me or my client?" If you answer the former question with "me"(yourself), don't do it! The wrong choice may result in action that can harm your client, who is not responsible in any way for the presence of danger. It is your responsibility to keep aware and to stalk the risks and dangers of the profession, in all relationships with your client and other colleagues.

COMPETENCY

The attitudes of counseling could be seen to demand that you portray the super-human qualities of being able to feel another's feelings, love unconditionally, and pay attention with complete and unwavering focus. No one is fully competent at maintaining these attitudes without imperfection.

Judging your own competency

You are doing your client a disservice if you judge yourself too harshly for not being a perfect counselor. Your client may wonder how you can accept his or her imperfections if you can't accept your own.

Outside challenges to your competency

Your competency may also be challenged by other members of the team or institutions responsible for your client's rehabilitation. Challenges that come from outside yourself can make you feel that the sanctity of your intimate relationship with your client has been violated. Be careful to consider outside criticism of your work before you react too defensively, for you may alienate an important colleague in the rush to protect your autonomy from imagined assault. You can also adjust your work to comply with suggested input as long as you perceive it to be *in the service of your client.* It is your duty to be vigilant and carefully screen outside bids to control your relationship with your client—especially if you feel they may be more in the interest of maintaining the health of an institution than the health of your client. Be aware that challenging the source of your client's rehabilitation funding is risky and can result in the termination of your employment. If you must challenge your employer, be respectful and clear about how the changes you propose translate into better service for your client.

INTIMACY

The dangers of intimacy are well known if you have ever engaged in a close relationship with another. They all stem from a confusion of boundaries that tends to arise from our innate need to seek comfort in union with one another.

Objectivity versus intimacy

In my experience the profession of counseling would have you believe that you can create proper boundaries with your client through remaining a fully objective listener and partner in the counseling relationship. This advice is well meant but infers that you don't empathize. In my opinion it impossible to remain fully objective if you practice the attitudes of counseling put forth in the previous chapter.

Protecting yourself from your client's trauma

If complete objectivity is impossible to maintain, how can you protect yourself and your client from the dangers of taking on your client's trauma and projecting your own responses? One answer to this question is in the acknowledgment of your client's healthy response to loss. This includes paying attention to and supporting resistance to the oppression of loss (Wade, 1997,2000) and helping your client navigate the grieving process. Even though you act as an empathetic and loving friend to support your client's rehabilitation you must remember that it is *not your trauma and loss but your client's.* If you do not keep this distinct boundary in mind, you can become distracted by your own responses and deplete the energy that you are professionally committed to give to your client. Much has been written about this subject in counseling literature as investigation of counter-transference and vicarious trauma.

POWER

It is crucial that the rehabilitation counselor understand the balance and imbalance of power, because the very word "disability" describes a loss of power in a world where real manifestation of power translates directly to manifestation of ability.

Avoiding a dangerous viewpoint

It is dangerous to look at the therapeutic relationship as one in which you, the counselor, hold the power to help your client who has lost it. This perspective removes the responsibility for change from your client and gives it all to you. Knowing this, you must relate to your client as at least an equal helper in the rehabilitation process. In this light it is your job to draw out and support his or her healthy responses to trauma and life-changing loss of power. Remaining an equal partner with your client can also protect you from a debilitating loss of energy which you might experience if you see yourself solely responsible for therapeutic change in the life of another.

Chapter 8
The Building of Rapport

Rapport is the exchange of common ground through a mutually agreeable transaction of energy. No real therapeutic relationship can exist without it. Therefore its establishment must become the first order of business between you and your client. The successful building of rapport is dependent upon the good will of three entities: you, your client and your chemistry together.

YOUR INPUT INTO THE BUILDING OF RAPPORT

The will to establish and build rapport is influenced by your adherence to the attitudes of counseling and innate need as a human being to be with others. Observe and study your client's willingness to engage in relationship with you and put yourself forward accordingly.

The beginning of rapport

Rapport begins with feelings of attraction that you have for your client as someone you would like to know further. These feelings are evidence of your will to engage in a relationship.

As the beginning of rapport is crucial and does not usually allow time for leisurely study and observation, you must consciously heighten your sense of your client's response to you in order to gauge the intensity of your approach. Your client will be more inclined to begin the building of rapport if you meet him or her with a like level of emotion, interest, and personal power.

Maintaining rapport

Once rapport is established you can maintain it by continued attention to the qualities of attraction you felt upon your first meeting. This attention is akin to unconditional positive regard and must be foremost, even through periods of resistance to you and the process of rehabilitation.

Resistance

Resistance needs to be acknowledged as a healthy response to oppression, because it is an indication that your client is capable of choosing not to participate in activity that does not feel right for him or her (Wade,1997,2000). It can become a facet of rapport as a vital part of any dynamic relationship. Resistance is a cue to look at your input and that of your colleagues, to see if you need to make any changes in your approach to your client's program of rehabilitation. One of the best ways to maintain rapport is to acknowledge, support, and celebrate your client's responses, including resistance, to all aspects of his or her rehabilitation. This attention to process is a true indication of your willingness to listen and maintain open and honest communication.

YOUR CLIENT'S INPUT TO BUILDING AND MAINTAINING RAPPORT

It is your responsibility, as a counselor and professional, to approach your client with the will to establish rapport and develop a therapeutic relationship. It is not your client's responsibility. He or she is under no obligation to accept your presence in his or her life and is entitled to reject you based on any premise whatsoever.

There is no chance for rapport if your client does not accept you as his or her counselor. This is also true if you are fired from the job. A ground rule of the counseling relationship is that you work for your client who can fire you at any given moment.

RAPPORT IN THE CHEMISTRY OF RELATIONSHIP

Your will to build rapport, when joined with your client's, becomes a defining force of the give and take within the counseling relationship. In this context, rapport functions as an effective equalizer of power for it can only exist through the equal input of you and your client.

Chapter 9
Counseling Skills

Counseling skills are like the tools of any trade or profession. They can have intrinsic beauty in and of themselves, but are of no real value until they are employed in the manifestation of what they were created for. In this light the counseling tools of listening/observing, reflecting, role playing, pacing/matching and synthesizing must be fused with the counseling attitudes of empathy, unconditional positive regard, and undivided attention to have any purposeful meaning.

LISTENING

The act of story-telling is not only an intellectual arrangement of words that portray events and emotions but a motivated recreation of your client's multi-modal response to a life that includes trauma and disability. As such it demands that your powers of listening be tuned to all manifestations of that response. When you listen, you must pay attention to signals from the whole person and not just to the words. These signals give you important information about how your client is feeling so you can match your therapeutic input to best reflect, support, and validate the response to trauma and loss.

Listen to the body and its sounds

sighs, murmurs, creaks, groans, grunts, yawns, squeals, rasps, hoots, rumbles...

Listen to emotional expression through laughter and tears

giggles, cackles, smirks, guffaws, peels, bursts, howls, whimpers, whines, sobs, keens, shouts...

Listen to cadence and speed of delivery

fast, smooth, jerky, relentless, slow, halting, intermittent...

Listen to volume

loud, quiet, and in between…

Listen to quality of voice

open, clear, soft, breathy, mellow, tight, raspy, harsh, boisterous, explosive…

All listening is active

You and your client are closer in the act of listening than in any other context, for when one truly listens to another, both participate in the collective act of hearing each other both implicitly named in an immediate story—the story of relationship between you and your client. That relationship is sadly weakened by the roles we are seen to inhabit—you (counselor) as "listener" and your client as "teller." This black and white assignment of purpose infers a passive role for the listener and an active role for the teller. Nothing could be farther from the truth. It is my experience that all listening is active, including the listening that is only present to receive. In this type of listening your lack of verbal response can help your client learn from the process of telling his or her story.

Knowing when to speak by listening to your inner voice

You can cultivate an inner voice that will instruct you when to speak or not to speak. This voice is accessible to you through learning how to quiet your thoughts and tune in to your instincts about how to respond to another's needs. This is a process that is usually learned through any discipline of meditation that resonates with your inclinations and belief system. The act of listening to this voice while another is talking makes you an active participant in a dialogue, even when you choose not to speak.

It is your responsibility to seek the spiritual training necessary to get in touch with your inner voice. It is also your responsibility to study your client's behavior and learn when he or she needs to only hear himself or herself talk. This is most often during the expression of emotion generated by grief. If you are tempted to interrupt during such expression, search your inner voice for instruction. In my experience it can not misguide you if you combine it with the practice of empathy, unconditional positive regard, and undivided attention.

OBSERVING

Your can learn a tremendous amount about your client's state of health and comfort of self-image through observing the condition of his or her body. You can also add to your knowledge through observing choices of lifestyle and environment. It is important to remember that this observation is for the gathering of information only and *not* for the building of any value judgments about your client's way of being in the world.

Any questions that arise about your client's physical health and safety must be openly discussed and referred to the appropriate colleagues. True observation can be a very effective tool for following and charting your client's progress and response to therapy. As with listening, it gives you the ability to better support and validate your client.

Observe posture

straight, open, loose, relaxed, tight, closed, coiled, rigid, fixed...

Observe motion

controlled, smooth, agile, fluid, frozen, stiff, trembling, agitated, jerky, disjointed...

Observe breath and body odor

sweet, clean, appropriately-perfumed, sour, rank, over-perfumed, influenced by toxic substances...

Observe eyes and gaze

clear, open, steady, sparkling, muddy, bloodshot, lidded, closed, flat, rolling, pop-eyed, teary, dry...

Observe the skin

vibrant, rosy, creamy, warm, smooth, flushed, chalky, ruddy, oily, sweaty, dry, flakey, dead...

Observe grooming

(Hair): Bare headed, covered (hat or other head covering), natural, dyed, clean, healthy, lustrous, brushed (combed), styled (decorated), dirty, matted, flat, falling out, unkempt…(Body hair: clean shaven, unshaven, bearded (long/short, trimmed/untrimmed)…

Observe clothing, shoes, and accessories

(clothes): Clean, ironed, color coordinated, modest, alluring, appropriately dressed, dirty, rumpled, stained, clashing colors, inappropriately dressed (for climate or situation)…
(Shoes): New, clean, well-worn, worn-out, dirty, repaired, un-repaired…
(Dress) how formal?, work related (what kind?), recreation (what sport or activity?), style (new/old, in-style, out of style)…
(Accessories, including jewelry/tattoos/piercings): unadorned, moderately-adorned, over-adorned, symbols (identification with specific group, subculture, social context, or belief system?)…

Observe state of home environment, furnishings, art and decoration

Warm, hot, cold, dry, moist, clean, dirty, good repair, broken down, cluttered, sparse, drab, colorful, in-style, out of style, tasteful, tasteless, art, no art, mementos or photographs, no mementos or photographs, evidence of creative activity, functional tools and appliances, old or broken tools and appliances…,

Observe presence of plants or animals (if any)

Neglected, tended, sick, healthy, pampered, friendly, hostile, well mannered, cowering, overbearing…

Make your own list

The above is a partial list of what there is to listen to and observe while being with another, for the signals we put out to each other are infinitely varied and highly complicated. *Make your own list of all you can think of to listen to and observe* while being with another, and keep in mind how it is affecting your interpretation and reflection of your client's story telling. Listening and observing are not skills for judging your client or decoding his or her stories, but for enhancing your response to them as a counselor and provider of therapeutic services.

REFLECTION

You will find that your client may need you to participate in the telling of his or her story through your reflection and verbal feedback. This type of participation is a vital form of therapy, where you become a mirror for your client through your genuine response to his or her story. As there is no prescribed format for this activity, you need to be tuned to the moment, through listening and observation, to be able to respond with appropriate questions and comments. You must respond honestly if you wish to maintain the rapport and trust you have labored to build. It is a victory for your relationship if your client challenges your response as it opens up dialogue that can strengthen his or her level of authority and self-knowledge.

ROLE PLAYING AND IMMEDIACY

You can create and model the semblance of real life in session with your client by taking the role of someone he or she needs to communicate with, or by creating the emotional dynamics of a difficult situation he or she needs to work through. This is often subtle work, where you draw out and practice healthy responses through your immediate relationship with your client. This is called immediacy and is both one of the most effective and dangerous tools you can use in the process of counseling.

Immediacy

Immediacy demands your strict adherence to the attitudes of counseling with special care to maintaining an objective boundary that keeps your interaction restricted only to the counselor-client relationship. Immediacy is only effective when your client makes the connection with his or her problem and you can weaken the therapeutic process by your pointing it out too soon.

PACING AND MATCHING

We each have our own unique rhythm and way of being in the world. This may be inborn or a response to life experience (including trauma and disability) or, more likely, a combination of both. Regardless of the source, we are most honored when others relate with us at a familiar and comfortable pace.

It is your job as a counselor to mold your responses to meet your client's pace as closely as possible. This is a complex task, which begins with observing your client's physical rhythms and feeling them pulse within yourself. Once you have synchronized your physical rhythms with your client's, you need to study and learn his or her speed, rhythm, manner of speech, and thought processing. These attributes are often affected by trauma and disability. One good source of information about your client's modes of processing can be found in neuropsychological and discharge reports from acute care rehabilitation institutions. These institutions can provide confidential reports that will be released to you if you ask for them through the proper channels with your client's permission.

Do not crowd your client with your interpretations of his or her pace, but use them to enhance rapport and empathy. Your client will be more inclined to accept your input and reflections if he or she feels that you are naturally respecting and matching his or her pace. A forced application of matching and pacing can contribute to counselor fatigue if you expend too much energy *trying* to follow your client. It is better to let your client create the pace and naturally *surrender* to his or her mode than to think too much about it and consciously impose it on yourself.

Time management

The skill of pacing also includes your management of the time you are allotted with your client. In the best of all possible worlds, you would have as much time with your client as you and he or she discover and agree you need to reach a satisfactory resolution of the therapeutic relationship. It is your job to balance the reality of any time constraints against your mutual need to complete a therapeutic cycle. You can meet this responsibility by gauging your client's level of dependency on counseling and consult him or her about termination of services in a manner that is proportionate to that need. This consultation process must be shared with all colleagues responsible for your presence, to insure as smooth a transition as possible.

SYNTHESIZING

Synthesizing is the most sophisticated and intricate skill of counseling. It requires that you instantaneously join the knowledge gained from observing and listening to your client with your intuition and feelings as a conscious member of a therapeutic process. It is rigorous work and usually recognized as a quality rather than a skill due to its unique and indefinable nature. Like other tools and attitudes of counseling, it is only meaningful to therapy when used in the service of your client. The clearest way to practice synthesizing is to open yourself to your analytical thought processes during therapy without letting them distract you from being able to keep undivided attention on your client. Synthesizing can bring you closer to your purpose of truly knowing and supporting your client through the experience of epiphany.

Epiphany

Epiphany is a moment of conscious coalescence when all the signals you have been sensing, learning, and paying attention to come together in a pattern that provides the answer to a fundamental question about your client. It is the fruit of synthesis, and not so much a tool in itself as it is the act of creating a useful setting in your mind for more efficient application of your attitudes and skills. A regular unfolding of epiphanies is a welcome event and is dependent upon the skillful use of synthesis.

Though your epiphanies are generated by your process, the temptation is to immediately share them with your client in the hope that he or she will be as excited about them as you are. This is not always a good idea and runs the risk of robbing your client of his or her own insight. It is best to limit your epiphanies to the enhancement of your own understanding and share them with your client, at an opportune moment by listening to your inner voice.

Chapter 10
The Counseling Environment

In rehabilitation work the counseling environment is dependent upon your client's freedom of mobility and ability to feel comfortable in the world outside of his or her private space. The choice of setting should be agreed upon by your client, you, and your case coordinator. Each setting has different requirements and advantages.

INSTITUTIONAL SETTINGS

Clients who have to be counseled in acute or long-term care institutional settings are usually seen, for one-to-one sessions, in their rooms or private offices within the institution. Sometimes they can be taken to public spaces, within or without the institution, for more informal work. Always make sure to clear your presence in the institution with the proper authorities and be sure you are welcome and expected to work at pre-arranged times and places. Also make certain to learn and carefully follow all checkout and return procedures if you are taking your client outside the institution for any reason.

Private rooms

Remember that a private room within an institution, no matter how personalized, is a long way from the pre-injury home environment where your client maintained a high level of individual or shared autonomy. Nevertheless it is important to treat a private space with the utmost respect for it is, at the moment, the only place where your client can begin to claim autonomy. You may have to respectfully educate other staff to this fact if your client has any complaints of his or her private world being violated in any way by employees of an institution.

Other private settings within the institution

Sometimes you can be given a seemingly neutral environment within an institution to hold an individual session. This can be an office or meeting room that does not reflect your choices or those of another individual. It does, however, reflect the choices and personality of the institution. This can be seen as a builder of rapport and equalizer of power between you and your client, for you are both guests of a seemingly larger and impersonal power. Being in this kind of setting also gives you the possibility to explore your client's responses to the character of the institution. These responses may open the door to expressions of gratitude for helpful treatment, or resistance to oppressive treatment. These positive or negative expressions are invaluable opportunities to rebuild your client's self-image as a free individual who is responding to but not identified with the structure of the institution.

OFFICE ENVIRONMENTS

Your counseling office

Your private counseling office is not your client's environment, nor should it pretend to be. Most counseling offices are designed to be as comfortable, neutral, and inviting as possible. But no matter how hard you try to present a neutral environment, you cannot conceal that it is not your client's personal space. It is *yours* to share. This is not a bad thing, but evidence of your presence in your own environment. Your choices in color, furnishings, photographs and mementos may be prevalent as reminders, to yourself, of who you are and how you fit in the world. It is important to observe your client's level of comfort in your office and make any adjustments to the environment (e.g., placement of furniture, removal of disturbing pictures or objects), if possible, to accommodate his or her wishes.

Someone else's office

If you are seeing your client in someone else's office, be aware that it is foreign to both you and your client. It is the personalized environment of another professional and will contain choices in decoration and mementos that are a reflection of his or her personal presence. This type of environment can have an equalizing effect on your relationship with your client as you both strive to be yourselves under the influence of someone else's choices.

IN THE CLIENT'S HOME

The best arrangement for learning about your client is to hold your sessions, if possible, in his or her home. This is where his or her personality is most evident, in chosen surroundings and mementos that are shrines to pre-injury life including hopes and dreams.

It is extremely important to remember that you are a guest in your client's home, and to comply with any and all requests he or she may have concerning respect of the environment. You are not expected to immediately know everything about the rules of the house and will probably commit a few errors of conduct during your learning process. Be gracious in your self-acceptance during this learning process for your client will probably be more forgiving of your mistakes than you are. Again, remember that he or she might have a harder time forgiving himself or herself if you cannot forgive yourself for a relatively minor transgression of protocol.

Working in a client's home also allows you to observe, over time, how he or she is practicing self-care through grooming and housekeeping. Self-care is an important reflection of return to health and can portray a positive or negative self-image through the energy displayed in building, providing, and maintaining a welcoming and self-nurturing environment.

Another great advantage of seeing your client in his or her home is the opportunity it provides for you to be treated as a guest. When you allow yourself to be your client's guest you are reversing the inherent power dynamics of the therapeutic relationship.

Do not hesitate to receive your client's hospitality, if offered, for it is extremely important to the restoration of self-image to be able to share his or her home with you. The worst you may encounter in gaining this invaluable therapeutic ground is secondary smoke, bad coffee or a stale cupcake.

Chapter 11
Care of the Counselor

Though we sometimes tire and feel run down during the rigors of our work as counselors, I do not believe that it is the relationship with our clients that causes counselor fatigue. Counselor fatigue is usually a response to trying to work within systems that do not honor and support the positive communication that exists within healthy relationships. These systems often impose unrealistic time constraints or prejudicial definitions of diagnosis and roles, which are created to support the healthy continuance of the institution itself and not clients and counselors.

A mechanism for overcoming the fatigue that is inherent within most of the systems provided for you to work in is to concentrate on your relationship with your client. This is best done through revisiting the attitudes of counseling.

REVISITING THE ATTITUDES OF COUNSELING

It is helpful to constantly stay connected to the attitudes of counseling. Empathy *expands* your world through placing you in that of another, regardless of its nature. Unconditional positive regard *enhances* your environment through the appreciation of your client in his or her highest light. Undivided attention *expands* your reality through giving you a passport to explore your client's world.

Empathize with yourself

Be in touch with *your own* feelings, even when your are empathizing with another. When you are relating with another in empathy it is your feelings that you are feeling through—not the other person's. Your feelings need to be acknowledged and nurtured (on your own time) to maintain the strength necessary to remain healthy in the counseling relationship.

Seeing yourself with unconditional positive regard

Maintaining an attitude of unconditional positive regard demands that you be able to see yourself in the same positive light that you see your client. If you see and treat yourself with the highest regard, you are practicing a level of consciousness that automatically promotes self-care and creates a positive therapeutic environment. It also implies that you must love yourself before you can love others—a tall order in a world that separates love of self from love of others.

Paying yourself undivided attention

It is important to treat yourself with the same respect with which you treat your clients. This includes paying undivided attention to your own need to grieve your losses and express joy.

GRIEVE YOUR LOSSES

You are human and, like all humans, suffer losses that you need to heal from. Some of these losses are past and some present. You must give yourself the time and space to acknowledge and experience the emotions of the grieving process (anger, sadness, fear, shock, guilt, denial, and hope) before you can accept your losses. You might not be able to do this work alone, and may do well to find a counselor or friend to help you through it. *Do not consider your client as a candidate for this job,* as he or she did not sign up to be your counselor, even though there is a degree of friendship in the counseling relationship.

DO THINGS THAT FEEL GOOD

Search out and give yourself time to do things that make you feel good. These can be personal, physical, creative, or spiritual activities and may include formal or informal group activities with like-minded people. This is an extremely important part of self-care and relies on your making time for it in your schedule regardless of how busy you are. Don't forget that one of the most nurturing things you do for yourself is to serve your client as a whole and healthy member of the counseling relationship.

Chapter 12
Hopes and Dreams

When the "client" part of the counselor/client relationship ceases to exist, your client becomes an "ex-client" and you, the "counselor," remain a friend. The relationship between you and your client does not disappear as soon as funding dries up or allotted sessions have run their course. Its remains are not only found in old file cabinets waiting to be destroyed after a prescribed number of years. You live on in each other's hearts and become part of each other's story as long as you live.

STAY IN TOUCH

It is gratifying to remain in contact with your client long after therapy has ended. Christmas and holiday cards are recommended, along with the occasional informal visit when it suits your mutual inclinations and schedules. You may hear of your client through future communication with colleagues you have been involved with concerning his or her care.

THE RELATIONSHIP LIVES ON IN SPIRIT

Your continuing hopes, dreams, and prayers for your client's future are a real and invaluable part of the therapeutic process, and can continue to affect you and your client long after your professional relationship is over.

REFERENCES

This collection of references is included to give you the opportunity to further explore writings that have influenced my philosophy and practice of counseling. It is purposefully eclectic and contains works from counseling, etymology, literature, and art.

Caetani, S. (produced by Heidi Thompson). (1995). *Recapitulation.* Vernon, B.C. Canada: Goldstream Books.
Demonstrates the use of creative art as a valid therapeutic response to trauma.

Carter, F. (1976). *The education of Little Tree.* University of New Mexico Press.
Celebrates the triumph of family bonds and cultural wisdom over trauma and oppression.

Corsini, R.J.&Wedding., D. (1995). *Current psychotherapies* (5th ed.). F.E. Peacock Publishers, Inc.
Provides authoritative and concise information about most important modern theories and systems of counseling.

Hesse, H. (1949). *Magister Ludi, The bead game.* Picador U.S.A.
Recreates the experience of true self-actualization and healthy self-image in a complex and demanding world.

Jung, C.G. (1963). *Memories, dreams, reflections.* Pantheon Books.
Allows participation in the discovery of original psychological understanding.

Krober, T. (1961). *Ishi in two worlds: A biography of the last wild Indian in North America.* University of California Press.
An affirmation of the resilience of the human spirit.

McGoldrick, M. (1982). *Ethnicity and family therapy*. New York: Guilford Press.
Gives insight into the unique ways that different cultures relate to universal aspects of human nature.

Mills J., & Crowley R. (1986). *Therapeutic metaphors for children and the child within*. New York: Brunner/Mazel Inc.
Highlights the importance of story-telling and metaphor as a most effective therapeutic tool.

Mogerman S. (1994). The discovery and use of shape therapy. *Counseling in the 21st century*. Vancouver, B.C. Canada.
Shares the discovery and use of a therapeutic tool based on human beings' ability to resonate with shapes.

Partridge, E. (1958). *A short etymological dictionary of modern English*. New York: Random House.
An invaluable reference that traces our language back to its original intention.

Rogers, C.R. (1951), *Client-centered therapy*. Boston: Houghton Mifflin.

Sacks, O. (1984). *A leg to stand on*. New York: Harper Collins.
An edifying personal account of trauma and recovery

Sachs, O. (1998). *The man who mistook his wife for a hat and other clinical tales*. New York: Simon & Schuster.
Demystifies the science of neurology through fascinating clinical stories.

Schaefer-Simmern, H. (1950). *The unfolding of artistic activity*. Berkeley, CA: University of California Press.
Correlates the development of individual human creativity over a lifespan with the history of art.

REFERENCES FOR PROCESS ORIENTED MEMORY RESOLUTION

Tanaka, M. (personal communication, San Mateo, California, Nov. 2003): For more information on Dr. Tanaka's work visit her website at http://www.marikotanaka.org

Baum, B. (1997). *The Healing Dimensions.* Tuscon Arizona: West Press.

Mindell, A. (1985). *River's way.* Boston: Penguin.

Watkins, J., & Watkins, H. (n.d.). *Ego states theory and therapy.* Boston: Penguin.

REFERENCES FOR RESPONSE BASED THERAPY

Wade, A. (1997). Small acts of living: Everyday resistance to violence and other forms of oppression. *Journal of contemporary family therapy.*

Wade, A. (2000). *Resistance in interpersonal violence: Implications for the practice of therapy.* Doctoral dissertation, University of Victoria, Victoria, B.C., Canada.

Todd, N., & Wade, A. (2003). *Coming to terms with violence and resistance: From a language of effects to a language of responses.* In T. Strong &D. Pare (Eds.), *Furthering Talk: Advances in the Discursive Therapies* (Chapter 9). New York: Kluwer Academic/Plenum.

Dr. Wade (whose works are referenced above) lives in Cobble Hill, British Columbia, Canada

About the Author

Sol Mogerman M.Sc. is a Registered Clinical Counselor in private practice in Victoria, British Columbia, Canada. He is on the staff of Kia Ora Rehabilitation Services, teaches at City University, Vancouver Island Campus, and is the author of *Objects in Mirror are Closer Than They Appear (Inside Brain Injury)*.

Index

A

abandonment 78, 136

acquaintance 127, 135, 136

addiction/addictions counselors 132

advocate 39, 42, 126, 130, 133, 140

affirmation 79, 166

alcohol 132

altered states of consciousness 144

ancestor 142, 144

angel 9, 11, 106, 144

anger 4, 17, 22, 23, 28, 37, 39, 46, 48, 49, 57, 59, 61, 64, 66, 68, 70, 74, 79, 81, 88, 91, 96, 98, 99, 102, 103, 132

animals 143, 156

art 3, 11, 13, 27, 83, 128, 142, 143, 156

art of friendship 4

assessment 27, 33, 89

attachment 20, 78

attitude 3, 22, 39, 60, 75, 89, 117, 122, 124, 125, 132, 133, 140, 145, 148, 149, 151, 153, 157, 159, 163

autonomy 149

award 29, 94

B

Bandler xix

body 6, 16, 32, 44, 81, 101, 125, 153, 155

body hair 156

body movement(s) 6, 21, 99

body odor 155

body work 4, 125

boundary/boundaries 4, 13, 16, 17, 28, 60, 77, 81, 83, 119, 131, 132, 136, 144, 149, 157

brain injury 3, 6, 8, 14, 15, 16, 17, 19, 21, 22, 25, 31, 62, 64, 71, 81, 90, 119, 131

breath 155

British Columbia 118

brother 5, 9, 12, 14, 15, 22, 25, 29, 35, 41, 43, 46, 59, 61, 63, 66, 70, 73, 76, 90, 91, 96, 139

Buddhist 142

C

Caetani, Sveva xix, 166

Canada 8

career 63, 104, 129, 130, 131

caregiver 29, 59, 90, 124

case manager 118, 119, 129, 131

chant/ing 23, 41, 78, 92, 94, 95, 101, 142, 144

chemistry 3, 152

child 6, 7, 9, 12, 13, 15, 17, 19, 20, 22, 25, 28, 38, 39, 49, 50, 52, 57, 58, 61, 66, 69, 70, 72, 73, 75, 77, 79, 83, 85, 86, 87, 89, 91, 98, 99, 101, 103, 104, 108, 110, 111, 112, 128, 137, 146

childlike 6, 48

Chorea 6, 113

Christmas 110, 165

clothes 37, 75, 87, 156

clothing 37, 128, 156

cognitive 27, 37

colleague 3, 112, 120, 121, 122, 127, 132, 135, 136, 137, 139, 140, 142, 143, 144, 145, 148, 152, 155, 158, 165

common sense 124

compassion 16, 37, 44, 120, 123, 124, 131, 134, 137, 139

compensation 128, 133
competency 148
confidentiality 4, 120, 124, 128, 136
conservator 15, 29, 35, 43
consult/consultation 35, 42, 90, 96, 120, 122, 123, 126, 128, 129, 132, 134, 139, 142, 158
Corley, Bob xix
Costello, Joan xix
counseling environment 63, 160
    client's home 162
    institution 161
    office, private 161
    office, shared 161
counselor-client 24, 157
creative activity 156
    art/s 143
    endeavor 143
    processes 142, 143
    teachers/therapists 143
    triumph/s 143
creative reminiscence 3, 121

D

dance/r 5, 6, 12, 14, 142, 143
dementia 6, 96
dentist/dental 42, 43, 64, 77, 123
depression 6
doctor/s 9, 23, 25, 42, 44, 56, 58, 76, 122, 124

E

Ellis, Albert xix
emotional
    attitude 133
    charge 90
    connection 135
    control 27, 68
    dynamics 157
    expression 7
    landslide 67

liability 21
maturity 140
output 21
pain 136
response 137
scale 25
stability 9
stable personality 81
state 20, 68
storm 57
vacillation 25
empathy 120, 121, 124, 145, 146, 153, 158, 163
epiphany 26, 159
Erikson, Eric H. xix
Erikson, Milton H. xix
ex-friend/s 136
ex-partner/s 138
extended care 5, 127
extrapolation 146
eyes 7, 11, 22, 27, 44, 60, 64, 68, 77, 100, 155

F

family 17, 25, 28, 33, 35, 37, 41, 43, 46, 48, 50, 55, 58, 63, 64, 66, 74, 76, 77, 80, 83, 90, 94, 96, 102, 105, 119, 128, 129, 136, 137, 139, 143
family counselor 82
family funds 128
fatigue (counselor) 147, 158, 163
fine motor control 24
food 49, 87, 111, 128
forgiveness 70, 73, 76, 80
Freud xix
funding 87, 129, 133, 149, 165

G

genes/genetic 6, 40, 82, 101
gift/s 15
God 80, 142, 144

government/support 118, 127, 128

grief/grieving process 3, 4, 6, 13, 17, 21, 28, 34, 67, 73, 91, 92, 102, 108, 132, 137, 140, 143, 149, 154, 164

group 144

   activities 164

   age 98

   experience 132

   leaders 132

   non-profit 119

   peer 124, 135

   spiritual 142

   support 118, 127, 135

   therapy 132

Guthrie, Arlo 104

Guthrie, Woody 8, 106

H

health/healthy

   alternative 125, 126

   care 39, 118, 122

   conditions 39

   mental 149

   needs 42, 118

   professional/s 42, 107, 122, 123, 124, 127, 131, 136

   psychological 3

   relationship/s 108, 136, 163, 164

   response/s 14, 150, 152, 157

   self-image 40, 50, 136, 162

   society 59, 118

   spiritual 7, 145

   state of 9, 49, 55, 75, 80, 149, 155

Hewitt, Kirk xix

Higgins, Terry xix

Hindu/ism 142

holistic 129

home care 15, 29, 54, 55, 64, 78, 89, 96, 111, 118, 127

   nurse/s 54, 124

housing

   shelter/housing 39

Huntington's disease 5, 6, 7, 8, 12, 14, 16, 18, 20, 22, 25, 28, 40, 44, 56, 63, 64, 73, 81, 96, 100, 101, 104

hygiene 43, 125

I

immediacy 157

independence 22, 99, 129, 134

independent wealth 128

individual 119, 144, 160, 161, 167

inner voice 154, 159

institution 31, 118, 123, 125, 126, 127, 129, 134, 148, 158, 160, 161, 163

insurance 14, 27, 29, 49, 87, 118

Insurance Corporation of British Columbia 118

intimate/intimacy 123, 124, 129, 137, 144, 148, 149

Islam/ic 142

J

Jesus 19, 23, 81, 92, 101, 142

job

   coach/s 130

   coaches 130

   counselor/s 117, 123, 126, 158

   specialist 131

joy 26, 67, 81, 110, 164

Jung, Carl G. xix

K

karma 86

keepsake/s 9, 11, 143

Kubler-Ross, Elizabeth xix

L

law

   enforcement/personnel 133, 134

   protection 134

suit 14, 74, 94, 112

tort 133

lawyer/s 9, 15, 20, 25, 33, 50, 55, 62, 70, 74, 76, 90, 94, 119, 127, 133

legal

advance 119

battle 90

claim 118

duty 128

guardian 9, 14, 35

permission 54

system 94

listen/er/ing 22, 27, 52, 71, 74, 83, 98, 101, 124, 144, 152, 153, 154, 156, 157, 159

active 154

objective 149

M

Mack, Tim xix

Maddess, Ralph xix

magic/cal 7, 92, 94

mantra/ 101

mantra/s 23, 63, 79, 81, 85, 92, 94, 98, 103, 144

matching 23, 113, 153, 158

May, Rollo xix

medicine men/women 142

medicine/medical 6

medication 21, 42, 43, 54, 55, 56, 60, 73, 79

medicine bag 111

problem/s 42, 123

profession 123, 126

records 122

reports 8

specialist/s 131

support 42

support worker/s 124

technicians 123

testing 119

therapy/ies 124, 126

training 124

treatment 43, 122, 124

Western 126

meditation 142, 154

memento/s 156, 161, 162

memory 4, 6, 8, 18, 19, 37, 56, 85, 138

mental/ly

health professional 127, 131, 132

impaired 22

specialist/s 131

state 125

Miller, Raymond xix

minor/s 128

Mogerman, Sol 167

Mohamed 144

motion 108, 116, 155

movement 80

movement disorder 6, 43, 64

music 3, 16, 29, 63, 85, 142, 143

N

natural healing process 6, 63, 126

neuropsychological examination/report 37, 158

neuropsychologist 131

no-fault insurance 119

non-profit 118, 135

North America/can 126, 142, 166

nurse/s

home care 124

institutional 123

public 54

nurture/ing 24, 90, 123, 140, 164

O

objectivity/observation 149

observing/observation 27, 59, 155

occupational therapist 101, 129, 135

odor 155

office
  counseling/professional 161
  someone else's 161
  within institution 161
one-on-one 125, 130
optometrists/opticians 123
outreach group 118

P

pacing 153, 158
paranoia/paranoid 14
paranoid/paranoia 6, 29
parent/s 20, 35, 59, 75, 77, 84, 85, 90, 137,
  138, 139, 140
peer group 124, 135
person centered therapy 63, 145
photograph/s 8, 11, 18, 25, 35, 39, 99, 143,
  156, 161
physiotherapist/s 122, 125
Piaget, Jean xix
plants 142, 143, 156
police 31, 61, 62, 69, 96, 102
positive 39
  change 39, 40, 70, 71, 78, 85, 101, 113,
    120, 127
  communication 161, 163
  connection 124
  environment 163, 164
  feelings 36
  growth 145, 146
  influence 143, 144
  momentum 59, 75
  nature 40
  perception 79
  relationship/s 125
  response/s 122, 128, 142, 144
  self-image 4, 58, 73, 162
  support 70
post-traumatic stress 44
posture 155

power 24
  dynamics 162
  equalization of 152, 161
  imbalance 13, 24, 150
  magical 7
  symbols of 53
prayer 142, 144, 165
prejudice 31, 142
private room/setting 160
probation 75, 106, 107
Process Oriented Memory Resolution
  (POMR) xix
projection/s 29, 79, 83, 112
protection 128, 133, 134, 139, 140
psychiatric disturbances 6
psychologist/s 17, 127, 130, 131
Punnett, Rod xix

Q

quality of life 3, 40

R

rage 9, 11, 13, 17, 21, 22, 28, 39, 46, 68,
  69, 72, 96
rapport 16, 39, 151, 152, 157, 158, 161
records/reports 8, 9, 12, 27, 41, 90, 108,
  122, 127, 128, 136, 158
reflection 6, 23, 25, 50, 59, 81, 85, 136,
  145, 156, 157, 158, 161, 162, 166
rehabilitation
  benefits/funds 87, 118, 119, 129, 133,
    149
  coordinator 127, 129, 130
  counselor 31, 63, 117, 118, 119, 120,
    125, 126, 129, 131, 133, 146, 149,
    150, 160
  department 8, 118, 129
  funding 129
  institution/hospital 118, 123, 126, 148,
    158
  needs 118, 130, 131, 132

neuropsychologists 131
occupational therapist 129
physical 125
process 120, 130, 138, 139, 150, 152
professional/s 119, 129
program 127, 139, 152
team 119, 122, 131, 132, 138, 139, 140
therapy 3, 136
value of Canadian society 59
religion 142, 144
reminiscence 3, 4, 57, 63, 100, 138
resistance 140, 141, 149, 152, 161, 168
resources 19, 119, 127, 128, 135
Response Based Therapy xix, 168
reunion 113
ritual 12, 24, 28, 33, 142, 144
Rogers, Carl xvi, xix, 63, 120, 145, 167
role
    client 24, 50, 64, 73, 154
    counselor 118, 123, 145, 163
    reversal 54
role-play 3
role-playing 121, 153, 157
Routledge, Richard xix

S

sacred 6, 11, 15, 111, 142, 144
sadness 4, 17, 39, 50, 91, 164
safety 7, 43, 48, 58, 61, 70, 80, 108, 128, 155
Salvation Army 31, 50, 119
Satir, Virginia xix
Schaefer-Simmern, Henry xix, 167
school 57, 85, 127, 134
self-image 3, 7, 13, 20, 25, 40, 50, 62, 63, 64, 73, 85, 119, 123, 130, 136, 138, 155, 161, 162, 166
settlement 133
sex therapist 13, 131
sexual abuse 13

shelter/housing 11, 128
shrine/s 11, 13, 15, 25, 35, 39, 44, 49, 56, 72, 112, 162
singing/songs 23, 63, 67, 79, 81, 85, 94
sister 35, 81, 139
skin 155
Smith, Jeff xix
smoke/tobacco/smoking 5, 11, 12, 24, 83, 96, 104, 112, 162
social worker 127, 128, 129, 131, 135
society 59, 86, 118, 136
specialist/s 40, 122, 123, 124, 130, 131
spiritual/ality 7, 14, 23, 98, 119, 126, 137, 142, 143, 144, 145, 154, 164
spouse/partner 7, 9, 13, 22, 137, 138, 139
story 3, 4, 16, 22, 23, 35, 37, 44, 57, 66, 81, 83, 104, 117, 118, 144, 154, 156, 157, 165, 167
story-telling 3, 18, 153, 167
support
    group 118
    group/s 127, 135
    medical 42, 122, 123, 124
    system/s 37, 42, 43, 59, 70, 89, 118, 119, 128, 131, 134
    therapeutic 86, 112, 125, 132, 136, 156, 158
    worker 43, 106
    worker/s 127, 132, 136
    workers 8
survivor 3, 4, 8, 135
synthesis 159

T

Tanaka, Mariko xix
teacher/s xix, 142, 143
therapeutic riding 86, 112
time management 151, 158
transportation 125
truth/s 2, 5, 47, 50, 90, 142, 154

U

unconditional positive regard 145, 146, 147, 152, 153, 154, 163, 164
undivided attention 147, 153, 154, 159, 163, 164

V

victim 53, 62, 73, 119
vision 25, 61, 144
visualization 142
vocational counselor 127, 129, 130
vulnerability 17, 28

W

Wade, Allan xvii, xix, 5, 149, 152, 168
Wennesland, Reider xix
workplace 129
world view 126
writing 3, 27, 68, 142, 143, 166

Y

Yalom, Irwin xix

0-595-31587-9